The Art of Longsword Fighting

Teaching the Foundations of Sigmund Ringeck's Style

Benjamin J. Smith

Photographs by Play of Light Photography
Illustrations by Peter Smith

FRONTLINE BOOKS

First published in Great Britain in 2021 by
Frontline Books
An imprint of
Pen & Sword Books Ltd
Yorkshire – Philadelphia

ISBN 978 1 52676 898 8

A CIP catalogue record for this book is
available from the British Library.

Typeset by Mac Style
Printed and bound in India by Replika Press Pvt Ltd.

Pen & Sword Books Limited incorporates the imprints of Atlas, Archaeology, Aviation, Discovery, Family History, Fiction, History, Maritime, Military, Military Classics, Politics, Select, Transport, True Crime, Air World, Frontline Publishing, Leo Cooper, Remember When, Seaforth Publishing, The Praetorian Press, Wharncliffe Local History, Wharncliffe Transport, Wharncliffe True Crime and White Owl.

For a complete list of Pen & Sword titles please contact

PEN & SWORD BOOKS LIMITED
47 Church Street, Barnsley, South Yorkshire, S70 2AS, England
E-mail: enquiries@pen-and-sword.co.uk
Website: www.pen-and-sword.co.uk

Or

PEN AND SWORD BOOKS
1950 Lawrence Rd, Havertown, PA 19083, USA
E-mail: Uspen-and-sword@casematepublishers.com
Website: www.penandswordbooks.com

Contents

Disclaimer

I have written this book for competent teachers to use to improve their teaching. If you are not a competent teacher do not undertake to teach this material. You do so at your own risk, and I disclaim all responsibility for your actions and cannot be held liable for any mishaps or accidents that may occur.

About the Author

I began training in historical European martial arts (HEMA) in 2000 when I was seventeen while going to college. I joined the Association for Renaissance Martial Arts (ARMA) and spent most of the next eight years applying that organization's method. I left the ARMA in 2008 around the end of my MA program to pursue my own approach. In graduate school I worked with a small circle of friends, and during that time I also trained in, and was approved to instruct a Dao style by Robert Jay Arnold of the Xinzhu Bagua Association, part of the Taiwanese Martial Arts Alliance and the Tian Wu Dao, which teaches a branch of Gao-style Baguazhang.

I joined the Historical European Martial Arts Alliance in 2009 and began working seriously on my interpretations of Sigmund Ringeck's longsword teachings. I taught it to my friends, and at WSU's summer camp program Cougar Quest for four years starting in 2009 and ending in 2012. The kids received it very well all four years, often rating it as one of the best workshops offered at Cougar Quest. It was a pleasure working with WSU's staff, and I hope such offerings will become commonplace in years to come. In 2014 I came to Boise and founded my current group the Hilt and Cross, and I have been happily teaching here since then.

Acknowledgements

I want to offer my thanks to my family, and particularly to my wife Erin, who has supported me in this project for so long. I also wish to thank all my current and former students. I found their ideas, input, and feedback invaluable and many of the things I share in these volumes come from them. Thank you to Randall Boudwin, Emily Boudwin, Phillip Rhoemer, Catherine Rhoemer, Michail Fragkias, Casey Goldsmith, Cora Goldsmith, and Bill England, who have all been especially supportive of me and my work here at the Hilt and Cross, and who were willing to spend so many hours letting me use them as test subjects for many of the experiments that made this book possible. I also wish to thank Andrew Ulrich, Ben Weaver, and Kris Skelton, with whom I worked in Pullman. Thank you to Jacob Norwood, Stewart Fiel, Mike Chidester, and Robert Hyatt with whom I began my HEMA journey. I also wish to offer special thanks to my father and mother, Kent and Diane Smith, whose sound advice made this project manageable, and whose support made it possible. I would also like to, thank my brother for providing the illustrations. I also wish to thank the good people of Frontline Press, and Pen & Sword Books, who welcomed my submission. In particular, I wish to thank John Grehan, who proved instrumental in giving me this opportunity, and Lisa Hooson, Susan Last, and Martin Mace, who patiently helped me polish the project.

Introduction

I wrote this book as a tool for instructors and serious students to guide the way they teach Ringeck's style of the Liechtenauer tradition through its introduction and the Zornhau section, where the foundation of your students' style will be laid. I hope it will help people understand not only how to do the techniques, but how to teach them effectively, and why they should be taught in the order and manner I present here. Perhaps most importantly, I hope that this book will help people understand Ringeck's fighting style and pedagogy as a complete entity, and the theory and goals behind the way it was taught, so that they can faithfully emulate Ringeck as far as can be known.

I believe that the way this art is learned and practiced matters just as much as the correctness of the physical execution of the techniques. It shapes the psyche of the practitioner, and their ability to understand the context of the techniques, which in turn affects the effectiveness of the techniques in application, the speed of their progress, and the depth of learning achieved by the student.

I have studied historical sword styles from several different cultures academically for twenty years, and I have practiced three for just as long. In my studies I observed that the evidence of ancient training methods shows remarkably broad consistencies despite separation in distance, time, and culture. I also observed that modern martial arts styles, and the books on modern and early modern martial arts, which I define here as roughly from around 1600 on, took on very different forms than the books written by Renaissance and medieval martial artists who likely made more use of these skills in warfare, dueling, and self-defense. More importantly, I observed that this happened in many different places within the same time frame. I believe that the evidence from the manuals of these periods reflects profound differences in their methods of teaching. On the assumption that these distinctions were significant, and the result of important differences in context, rather than progress in teaching methods, I decided it would be worth my time to try to recreate as much of the thinking and pedagogy as I could. I derived it as strictly as possible from the evidence in the primary source material.

First, medieval and early Renaissance martial arts were taught with clear master-student relationships, with more experienced practitioners guiding the development of the less experienced very closely.[1] Second, and perhaps most importantly, these ancient arts seem to have been chiefly taught in a one-on-one context through carefully designed partner drills. We do not, for example, see many instances of long sequences of techniques to be done without an opponent, or for the practice of large bodies of men. Third, they used little in the way of safety equipment, except when they were training for combat in armor, and even then, we sometimes see a large amount of work out of armor using techniques which are probably intended for armored combat.[2]

The best-preserved martial arts which originate from before the 1600s are the Japanese *koryu*. These martial artists spend the vast majority of their time on intensive, pre-arranged, partner drills. They saw this as the primary teaching method because development of skill is best done in the presence of a teacher, with an opponent who is acting vigorously against you, but with a set of techniques that is fixed so that you can focus on perfecting a single specific aspect of your art in each drill. The arrangement of Ringeck's *fechtbuch*, and indeed virtually every other original historical European martial arts text for dueling, self-defense, or the battlefield, from before 1600, parallels these processes that we see in the *koryu* precisely.[3] While sparring, hunting, strength training, tournaments, and possibly test cutting, all played essential parts in the development of medieval and Renaissance warriors, it was this specialized kind of partner drilling that formed the core of their martial arts curriculum, and to which the majority of their texts are devoted.

Each drill should have a clear teacher and student. The teacher will be the person who loses the exchange if the student does their part correctly. The teacher sets up the context for the student to learn how to win, and adjust, or demonstrate the consequences of mistakes until the technique is learned thoroughly. I wish to point out that drills like these need to be done correctly, and in order, for the drill to reach its maximum potential as a training medium. If you approach a drill as a simple routine, just a bunch of steps to go through when you practice, your body might learn the motion, but your mind will not learn anything new, and it is likely that you will learn the technique incorrectly because its purpose and execution will not be clear. Each action in a good drill must be done with intention, with as much force, focus, speed, and power as you can muster, while staying safe. You and your training partner must push the limits of your control, and, if you do this, then each drill should be just as challenging as a sparring match while allowing you to focus on the lessons that the drill is designed to teach. The teacher must actively work to force the student to reach for perfection or fail. In an ideal world where you have all the desirable equipment, and choose to emphasize realism and martial effectiveness in your training, you will start with the sword sheathed, or simply held as if sheathed in the off-hand, draw, approach, attack or defend, if you stab pull the weapon out forcefully, and after the exchange withdraw to a safe distance while remaining on guard, and only then relax and then return the weapon to the scabbard. Each drill needs to be repeated thousands of times to build up the instinct to do it correctly. You do all of this so you can get used to treating the weapon realistically, establish the right mindset in your students, and learn the psychology of fighting with a sword.

Modern HEMA training should differ from ancient training methods in a few important ways. In the few records of the ancient training methods that survive to the present day, much of what the student was supposed to learn was left unsaid. They did this in a context that was different in three important ways. First, they knew a great deal that they did not feel they needed to bother saying. Second, ancient teachers depended on the loyalty of their students and this could not be guaranteed until one had known someone for a very long time. This colored their teaching by forcing masters to obscure or delay teaching certain things. While personal loyalty is important to us in the modern day, it has largely ceased to be a life and death issue. We do not need to place such deep trust in our students the way they did, so there is no need to keep secrets from them. Third, should the student come to the wrong conclusion, a skilled teacher who thoroughly understood their art could easily correct them. We must do so as far as we can while acknowledging the gaps in our knowledge. Fourth, our current state of expertise still leaves many questions, not only as to the precise method of execution for many techniques, but also pertaining to their role in the larger pedagogy and systems of strategy. This makes independent student efforts at inquiry valuable, and we cannot leave these things unsaid or questions unanswered. We should be explicit about everything we teach, why we teach it and where we got our information. We should be especially clear about what we do not know, and when and where we are guessing. We must encourage our students to become equally as active and thorough at sharing their learning and insights from their own inquiries. Devoting time to experimental activities, especially when questions come up naturally in the course of a lesson, usually yields worthwhile insights.

This volume presents the foundations of the longsword style of the Liechtenauer tradition, as taught by Sigmund Ringeck. For space reasons this includes only the general teachings, the section on the Zornhau, and its attendant introductory material. These sections of Ringeck's manual offer what I call a 'complete fighting style', with options for fighting virtually any technique, including aggressive grappling. I argue that these sections were designed to achieve two purposes. First, to quickly prepare a student to fight for real with a small set of techniques that they could easily adapt to new situations. Second, to provide a way to learn and teach the principles and skill sets crucial to developing high-level martial arts skills, including measure, footwork, timing, control, courage, sensitivity, intuition, and the value of precisely executed technique. I hope to offer more on the subject in future volumes.

I recommend reading the entire book all the way through at least once before starting to teach from it. This will allow you to become be familiar with all the terms and concepts, and understand the desired end result. I designed the book on the premise that the teacher would lead their students through the book one section at a time, one drill at a time, from start to finish. Though it is often helpful to reference later material when you are teaching earlier material to establish context, you should not skip around through the book's content in your practice. Ringeck intentionally introduces ways to defeat, or prevent, advanced techniques long before he teaches how to do them. This pedagogy operates on the premise that you and your students have learned the first lessons thoroughly before you approach the later lessons. There are assumptions built into the later lessons about your knowledge and skill sets, and it will be difficult to learn the later lessons effectively without them.

After the introductory sections I will use my own translation of the Dresden, Rostock, and Glasgow manuals. I owe a great debt to the work of others who have come before me in their study of the original texts and their generous offerings of their translations, particularly the works of Christian Henry Tobler, Dierk Hagedorn, David Lindholm and Keith Farrell. In my rendering of Ringeck's manuscript I have opted for clarity of meaning rather than a literal translation. This inevitably leads to some subtle inaccuracies, and I beg the linguists' patience with them. I feel that the meaning, and subtleties of the work, at times, become muddied in a literal translation, and I felt a translation that emphasized clarity would be the best solution for this particular project. Readily available literal translations and transcriptions of the original manuscripts can be found on the Wiktenauer website: http://wiktenauer.com, and I encourage all serious students to examine them as well. I'd like to offer my special thanks to the generous people who put so much time and effort into that website and its invaluable material, and I wish to encourage my readers to donate generously to support their work. I have done my best to note which manuals my interpretations come from when it differs from other works, and I beg the readers to forgive my errors when they inevitably find them.

My own writing in this book will appear in several kinds of sections labelled: 'Historical Context', 'Theory', 'Method', 'Drills', and 'Tips for Teachers'. Historical context sections will present background information from research on the time period, archaeology, museum studies, and examinations of artifacts, which may be relevant to how we understand Ringeck's art, or the language used by him or

Liechtenauer. I have tried to be sparse in these sections, as they are mostly for the curious, but they are on occasion important for understanding the book. The theory sections include a thorough analysis of individual sections of the original text, notes on the works I contrasted it with, experiments I did to arrive at the interpretations, and my justifications for my interpretive choices. These sections will establish how different portions of the manual fit together, and establish a clear curriculum and style for the modern practitioner. The theory sections will frequently reference works within and outside the Liechtenauer tradition that illuminate or contrast with Ringeck, and this is where you will find the 'Frog DNA' necessary to recreate an art like this, and I have done my best to be explicit about when and where I needed to pull from other sources. Method sections will explain in detail how to execute and teach particular techniques. Drill sections will present tightly choreographed drills for learning specific techniques and skills, as well other less choreographed activities, designed to build up the skills one needs in order to execute the techniques under pressure, including sparring, and variations on sparring. The sections entitled 'Tips for Teachers' explain common pitfalls in teaching this material to your students and how to help them learn the material more easily and avoid developing bad habits.

The system I'm offering in this volume builds up to flexible and unprepared sparring. Students begin by learning one strike. They learn the whole technique

---

The General Teaching   129

Drill: *Winding*

The attacker will be the student and the defender the teacher. The attacker approaches and cuts a *Zornhau*. The defender cuts a *Zornort*. The attacker then rolls their sword's long edge towards their opponent's weapon and lifts their arms, moving their blade up so that it is roughly parallel with the ground at the height of their face, aiming the point of their sword so they can stab them in the face.

Ben takes the role of the attacker and Randy will be the defender. Ben approaches and attacks with a *Zornhau*.

Randy responds with a small passing step back and strikes with a *Zornort*. This image depicts the moment the swords meet, just before Randy's weapon can threaten Ben's face. Ben feels that he has become weak in the bind and will start the *Winding*.

Ben begins his *Winding* by rolling the sword's long edge towards Randy's body, angling it up and out on a diagonal angle. In this position Ben will need to pull his point back just a tiny bit so that he can thrust, but this will not always be necessary. Emphasize that it is a real fight the thrust can begin before the winding has even been completed. The *Winding* should, ideally, attack as well as defend.

Ben finishes his winding holding the weapon just above his eye-line to protect his upper quarte, locking Randy's blade between the strong of his sword and his cross. Ben's sword is aimed squarely at Randy's face with a very slight downward angle. In a real fight, or a sparring match with helmets, Ben would thrust forward to complete the technique.

Typical pages.

---

130   The Art of Longsword Fighting

Tips for teachers: 'beginning to feel'

Unless you are training with someone who is very skilled and is deliberately trying to give only a certain kind of bind there is no guarantee in the first few months of training as to whether one student will be weak or strong at the sword or when they are supposed to be one or the other. This unfortunately means that we modern practitioners must practice the phases of the technique in a slightly different order than they are presented in Ringeck's manual. The following drill is designed to help students learn this core principle.

Drill: feeling the bind

This drill requires that all participants have established a strong level of control. In this drill there is no designated attacker or defender, but there will be a designated 'teacher' and 'student'. The participants will approach and strike *Zornhaus*. The teacher will simply make this first strike with force and intent and do nothing else. The student will feel the bind whether they are weak or strong and thrust with a *Zornort* or use *Winding* appropriately. Reset after the first reaction to the bind. Ideally the student should have scored a clear hit either with a *Zornort* or a *Winding*. If a clear hit was not struck then they read the bind wrong and need to reset. Do this from both sides.

It is of utmost importance that the blows be thrown at proper range and at correct targets. This is the number one thing the teacher should be trying to watch for at this stage. Many people do not get close enough to hit their opponent's head or body with their initial offensive strikes, or if they intend to cut with defensive strikes. You should not move on to this stage of training unless the previous material has been done correctly. If students begin making lots of mistakes in this drill, have them step back and relearn the previous material. The students may be overcompensating, over-

Ben approaches and attacks. Randy, playing the role of the teacher, will feel the bind to learn whether he is weak or strong, and respond either by thrusting with the *Zornort*, or *Winding*.

with its permutations from both the attacker and defender's side. Then they learn to do those with a non-compliant opponent. Then they learn to apply the technique without a designated attacker and defender. At this point they are sparring, but with only one set of techniques. Then they learn the next technique, go through the same entire process, and end by having limited sparring with two sets of techniques. This continues until they have learned the entire curriculum of Ringeck's teachings and can spar freely with the whole thing. If done properly, taking the time to ingrain and contextualize each technique, training on your own, and attending regluar practice, expect that this process will require at least a couple of years to complete the entire system, not just what is shown in this volume.

PART I

Core Concepts

Chapter 1

Sigmund Ringeck

Sigmund Ringeck, also known as Sigmund Schining ein Ringeck, and Sigmund Amring or Sigmund Einring, was *Fechtmeister*, and Schirmaister to one of the Duke Albrechts who was Count Palatine of the Rhine and Duke of Bavaria, and it is his work on the longsword that I interpret and teach. We do not know which of the Duke Albrechts he served, but he seems to have lived in either the late 14th century or the early or mid-15th century. He learned Liechtenauer's fighting style, and was listed as a member of the Society of Liechtenauer by Paulus Kal in his *fechtbuch* from the late 15th century. His titles indicate that he both served in the Duke's military organization and taught the fighting arts to its members. His last name, Ringeck, might possibly indicate that his family came from the Rhineland.[4] The exact time of the founding of Liechtenauer's style remains somewhat in doubt, with some researchers proposing that he founded the style in the late 14th century, and others favoring the early 15th century. I favor the latter interpretation of the evidence for two reasons. First, the production of manuals of the style occurs most prominently in the mid to late 15th century, not the early 15th century, and the dating of the supposedly earlier manuals is more doubtful. Second, the events which serve as the best candidate for prompting the establishment of the society would be the Hussite wars, for which several such martial societies were established in the early 1400s.[5]

My work draws on several extant versions of Sigmund Ringeck's treatise. The principal version I work from will be the MS Dresden C487 manuscript, which also contains several other works, and is currently held by the Sächsische Landesbibliothek in Dresden, Germany. Other copies of Ringeck's text can be found in Glasgow, Scotland, Rostock, Germany, and Augsburg, Germany, all of which have some differences from the Dresden version. I have found the Glasgow version very helpful as it has many beautiful illustrations, though unfortunately, none for the section interpreted here.

In his *fechtbuch* Ringeck provides insightful commentary on the meaning of the *merkverse* of Johannes Liechtenauer, the fight master who, according to Dobringer, after traveling extensively to learn the fighting techniques of many masters, created his own cohesive system for the longsword. Liechtenauer composed poetic verses to provide structure for his teaching and to aid his students in learning the system. The Dresden, Glasgow, and Rostock manuscripts include instructions for practicing other skills, many of them related martial arts, that were understood, taught, and practiced in conjunction with the art of fighting with the longsword in Liechtenauer's style, such as armored fighting with the longsword and spear, unarmored fighting with the sword and buckler, grappling, fighting from horseback in armor, unarmored fighting with daggers, and fighting with messers. If we take the simultaneous placement of these writings in a given source as evidence of their connectedness in teaching and presentation, and I argue that we should, then we should understand Liechtenauer's longsword art as only one among many arts that were taught by masters of this tradition. We know little about the compilers of these texts, but they probably were taught by masters of the tradition, or were connected to someone who was.

Many of Ringeck's contemporaries produced similar works that also explain the teachings of Johannes Liechtenauer. These can be found throughout Europe, and they constitute the single most documented longsword style that we know of to date. Ringeck's manuals offer perhaps the most complete set of instructions on Liechtenauer's teachings. He also included some of his own material at the end. Other masters used and referenced his manual long after him. In 1570 Joachim Meyer included a copy of Ringeck's teachings in his final manuscript, and Hans Medel von Salzburg created a new version of it, adding his own teachings and illustrations.[6]

The emphasis on dueling, formal or informal one-on-one combat to settle disputes, signifies at least two important points. First, one-on-one fighting on simple flat ground with similar, often identical, weapons, is the logical place to begin martial arts teaching, as dealing with multiple opponents, different terrain and obstacles, and cohesion of action as a unit, cannot be feasibly taught until one is able to deal with one opponent in a simplistic circumstance. Second, the simplified context of the duel can be readily built upon for learning self-defense, skirmishing, conduct in sieges, and open battle. While the records we have connected to the Liechtenauer tradition do not spend many pages on these other modes of fighting, I believe it logical to say that because these other forms of combat occurred frequently in the era, and because the writers of this tradition specifically mention the applicability of their arts in warfare, and because they often served in military forces, the work on dueling served as the pedagogical foundation for teaching these other arts. The context of other modes of combat emphasizes team efforts, and, therefore, more limited technique sets. The teaching of these other modes of combat probably emphasized working with a military unit in exercises, rather than the practice of techniques. Therefore, building from a technique set optimized for dueling makes a great deal of sense from the perspective of a martial arts teacher. In addition, these first lessons are the ones most likely to be broadly applicable in the various contexts of combat.[7]

There have been, to date, three prominent translations and interpretations of Sigmund Ringeck's fight book, and the attendant Liechtenauer tradition, published in English: Christian Henry Tobler's, David Lindholm's, and Herbert Schmidt's. These provide valuable interpretations, information, and insight into Ringeck's work and fighting techniques. What I will present here is a new interpretation that differs in the execution of many techniques from these previous works. I have also added my insights on how to transmit Ringeck's art to our students in a modern context. I use what I believe were the teaching methods for which we have the most evidence from Ringeck's book, research into other styles of the era, and other martial arts in general. There will be some notable nods to modern needs and sensibilities, which I try to be very plain about. I have attempted to lay bare my evidence and conclusions for each particular mode of practice and variation on the interpretations of techniques, and to lay out the sourcing of my conclusions about Ringeck's style of swordsmanship from extensive research into the various manuscripts that contain his teachings, and, when relevant, the work of Ringeck's contemporaries, as well as other fighting systems which illuminate his sometimes opaque teachings.

As the Dresden version of Ringeck's fight book has no illustrations, and those of the Glasgow version are occasionally cryptic, and because some of the material requires additional explanation beyond what Ringeck gives, especially in terms of teaching pedagogy and methodology, I have been forced to draw liberally on writings and art in other sources. I have tried to carefully cite their context and potential differences so that I can better explain Ringeck's art.

Ringeck's manuals give us one of the most complete and well-documented versions of Liechtenauer's teachings. His fighting style emphasizes direct aggressive strategy, controlling the opponent, fighting securely, and techniques for feeling the opponent's position and actions that make one's response time much faster than when one relies on their eyes alone, and more effective than when one relies on intuition alone. Liechtenauer provided one of the soundest and most popular Renaissance systems for fighting with a longsword. We enjoy practicing it very much at the Hilt and Cross, and we hope that you will find our work valuable.

Chapter 2

Ringeck's Fighting Style

This book teaches Sigmund Ringeck's interpretation of Liechtenauer rather than a synthesis of the masters of his tradition. I chose to do this because I prefer Ringeck's take on Liechtenauer, not because I do not value the works of Kal, von Danzig, Meyer and others. I do value them, and I have had to draw liberally on their works to complete this book. The differences between these teachers' works are often subtle, and they will receive their proper treatment in the relevant sections. Nevertheless, I feel it is important to explain that what you will see in the interpretation I offer here reflects what I understand as Ringeck's perspective rather than the teachings of other masters and writers from his tradition, a synthesis thereof, an attempt to recreate Liechtenauer's original fighting style, or an attempt to create a modern HEMA longsword system by combining multiple longsword styles from a broad historical and geographic context.

A fighting style includes a chosen set of techniques, strategies, training activities, psychological preparation, and weapon systems, which it uses to prepare a practitioner to achieve victory in combat. Ideally, this provides a way for a student of a style to learn how to control a fight, guide its direction, and ensure they come out on top, without injury to themselves. To do this, the teacher designing the style uses their chosen strategies to select their weapon systems and technique sets, the training activities to prepare their students to use those systems and techniques, and then guides the student's psychological preparation, so they can employ them under pressure.

A well-designed fighting style will select strategies, goals, training methods and techniques according to the context it was created for. A teacher of a fighting style must also decide what to leave out. In some ways this can prove more important than what they put in. One could, theoretically, document every single possible technique, and variation, and teach them all to a student. Doing so, however, would waste a great deal of time because many techniques would be redundant, and the more you choose to include in your style, the more time it takes to transmit it to your students. No teacher has that kind of time. Sometimes one does not have a great deal of time to impart this knowledge to a student, and if one cannot develop a student's skills quickly, then one's art will prove to be of little use to a student. A good teacher must decide which techniques will form the core of the style, which techniques they will teach to deal with niche situations, which techniques should be shown to the student so they know how to beat them with what they already know, but not so that they should train to do them, unless they will become teachers themselves, and which techniques should be left completely out.

As examples, Ringeck does not instruct his students to do any of the common long-edge rising cuts in his books, nor are there any long lunging thrusts in this style. Fiore does not include any vertical cuts in his style, relying solely on the diagonal cuts for downward strikes, nor does he deal with extensive winding techniques. Fiore omits the prominent high guards of the Liechtenauer system, where the sword is held above the head for example, or at the shoulder in a forward stance. Neither Ringeck, nor Fiore, includes anything substantial on ground fighting. I do not believe that they left these things out because they could not figure out how to do them. I argue that they left them out because these techniques had no place in their chosen strategies. They could already accomplish the things they were trying to do with the techniques that they already included. A truly great teacher must understand these stylistic choices, or they will fail to impart their style effectively to their students.

Leaving things out of a fighting style often seems counter-intuitive to a new student. Modern martial arts culture inherited a legacy of cross training in different martial arts, and my students often mention the success of mixed martial arts, and Bruce Lee's philosophy of learning what you can that is best from everywhere, as their frame of reference for this. This sometimes leads people I meet to delve only shallowly into a wide number of arts, rather than developing deep levels of effective skills. Much of their training can go to waste learning redundant techniques, and contradictory strategies. They do this without realizing that different martial arts can adopt completely different, even contradictory, approaches to fighting, but, for reasons of physical or cultural context, limitations of training methods, preferred outcomes, purpose, or just plain personal preference, these might both be completely valid approaches.

Ellis Amdur said that learning two styles faithfully was akin to having two wives, and devoting oneself properly to both is an insurmountable challenge for most people.[8] When Bruce Lee underwent his famous cross-training regimen he did so after becoming a master in an established tradition. This gave him preparation and context for assessing what to put in and keep out of the style he was developing. Dobringer reports that Liechtenauer did something similar, possibly as a journeyman, or as a professional soldier, but also possibly as a master in his own right. Most people who try to cross train extensively do not have this kind of preparation, and get mediocre results.

Now, it should be no secret that the martial arts of the world atrophied a great deal in the last 500 years. Most of them ceased to exist altogether in the face of the rise of large national armies and rapid technological advancement, and the survivors did not survive because they were the best, but because of isolation which insulated them from these influences, and cultural dedication to maintaining traditions. Nor did the survivors reach the modern era completely intact. Every style that I have researched has evidence of lost teachings. When I undertook to learn a Chinese martial art some years ago, after I had more than ten years of experience learning Ringeck's art, I could tell immediately that it had become disconnected from the context it was created for. There was too much solo training, not enough teaching on how each technique worked, not enough information for detecting when to choose to use different techniques, and no practice of cutting technique. I still found the experience extremely valuable, and many of the insights I have had into Ringeck I can thank my teacher, Robert Jay Arnold, for. I could tell that the art he taught me came from a powerful origin, but so much of what I needed to use it in the way I would use Ringeck's style would have to come from more research and practice on my own.

Disconnection from their historical contexts gives some surviving martial arts blind spots that sometimes yield odd results, hence my passion for learning ancient arts and their cultural contexts. When dealing with historical martial arts though, where good practice was an immediate life and death matter, it is, generally, pretty safe to assume that such blind spots would have been detected, and dealt with ruthlessly, and that when we find something that seems missing we should ask 'Why was this left out?' instead of assuming that the designer of the system overlooked something important. We should ask ourselves 'Is another technique already in the system dealing with the situation?' 'Is there a piece of historical or cultural context that made this unnecessary in the day?' 'Is another course of training in a different weapon system connected to the art I am learning covering this context?' 'Is there something we have not even discovered yet that answers these questions?'

For example, my students familiar with Brazilian Jiu-jitsu, Judo, and western wrestling consistently note the lack of groundwork in historical European grappling styles. Talhoffer's 1467 manual, for example, includes only four groundwork techniques: two of them are different ways to draw your dagger and stab your opponent in the head, and the others are escapes. The evidence for why this is the case cannot be easily found within the manuals themselves. We have to look hard at the historical, physical, and cultural contexts of the time to find out why this was. In terms of ancillary evidence from the cultures of the era, I cite that the languages of warrior cultures from all over the world almost universally link falling to the ground with death. In most languages 'he fell' is synonymous with 'he died', and the dead were known as 'the fallen'.

From experiments training and sparring with historical technique, we discover that staying on the ground, or intentionally going to the ground with someone, so you could grapple, choke them out, or break their limbs, takes much more time than the one or two seconds one can conveniently use in medieval or Renaissance combat contexts, where the possibility of multiple opponents with deadly weapons was concerned. Using a weapon like a dagger is more effective, quicker, easier to train, and has advantages for multiple contexts, that wrestling on the ground does not. Moreover, it could be assumed in those days that both you, and your opponent, would have a dagger, which changes the tactical decisions you can make. If a dagger was unavailable, then escaping from the ground so that you could fight normally would usually be a superior choice to ground fighting, because there might be another opponent coming at you with a weapon. The one exception to this from the era was formal duels in armor, which occasionally ended with daggers on the ground after some grappling.[9]

We need to do our best to make ourselves aware of the things we do not yet understand in our style. We will often need to discover the answers in sources other than the manual right in front of us. So be aware of this need, and do your best to find these questions, and answers for them.

While no single weapon system and fighting style will suffice for all possible contexts, training in any system and style will help prepare a student for all of the other contexts. The Kunst des Fechtens of Liechtenauer's tradition included a great deal more than just his longsword style. Books on fighting in the medieval and Renaissance traditions frequently have multiple sections, sometimes written by multiple authors, dealing with different weapon systems and types of fighting.

In the early Renaissance combat chiefly occurred in three contexts: warfare, duels, and self-defense, and the records of the period show us many different ways each of these could happen. Though Ringeck and Liechtenauer speak of warfare as a chief context for their larger style, they clearly designed this particular longsword art for unarmored dueling. This art of fighting with the longsword deals exclusively with one opponent, who is also using a longsword. They always assume in the longsword section, that you saw your enemy, and drew your weapon, before engaging them. This curriculum may have also served as a preparatory stage for training to fight in other contexts. The vast majority of the techniques in Ringeck's manuscripts, particularly in the early sections dealt with in this volume, will work in other contexts, and very few of the techniques would ever become liabilities, and even then, only in very specific circumstances which are easy to make a student aware of. Other parts of the books connected with this longsword style deal with armored combat, grappling, mounted combat, and other weapons and training, which would directly compliment this training. The larger cultural context, with frequent warfare, dueling, hunting, and large-scale tournaments, with their wide variety of activities, also lends credence to the idea that this particular art was only one of many connected activities that formed the warrior's preparatory training and culture. These facts lead me to believe that most students of this tradition probably learned quite a bit more than just this longsword art, and that, where possible, we should also similarly diversify our training among these systems.

The tradition of Liechtenauer's fighting style, the '*Kunst des Fechtens*', uses a very aggressive mindset, tightly focused on a specific tactical goal: to defeat your opponent with the fewest number of actions while not permitting them to hurt you. They taught their students to look at their opponent, see his openings, and attack in the safest and swiftest manner by choosing one of five strikes that best suits the position and distance. They emphasized continuous offense, and they taught that simply having the courage to strike first often won fights.[10] Superficial understanding of this mindset breeds recklessness. I argue, however, that Liechtenauer's style is not wildly aggressive. He and his students do not teach to attempt to exploit an opening at the cost of rendering yourself vulnerable. They constantly advise us to fight in ways that do not permit our opponent to get through with their own techniques.

Liechtenauer and Ringeck taught to attack, but to do so in order to gain control of your opponent, and safely defeat them. They built an attack into almost every defense, and the vast majority of their defenses are accomplished in a single motion. By constantly using actions that both attack and at the same time protect you, followers of this tradition keep the opponent watching what they are doing, while they themselves merely need to seek their opponent's next opening, and choose attacks they can trust to keep them safe.

Liechtenauer also offered a key insight into reading an opponent. He either knew from training he received, or discovered through his own experience, that the sense of touch is much more sensitive, and prompts quicker responses, than the sense of sight. If you would like to test this, then get a training partner and stand at a distance that requires you to merely reach out with your hand to make contact with your opponent, without moving your feet or bending forward. Then touch a pre-determined target on the other person. Begin with your hands at your sides and have the other person try to stop you from touching their chest or face. This should be very difficult, if not impossible. Then step back one pace so that you will have to step to touch your target. They should easily be able to stop that action with one motion. Then move back into the closer distance, have both of you extend your hands downward and let your wrists touch at a point midway between you. From this position try to touch the same target you did before. You will find that in spite of the fact that their eyes could not keep up in the first drill, and that even though the attacking hand starts a little closer to the target, they will be able to stop the attack much more reliably, because they have the feedback of touch. To develop this sensitivity to its fullest teachers in this tradition spent a significant amount of time teaching their students how to feel the way swords bind when they meet.

Liechtenauer's *Kunst des Fechtens* should, I believe, be taught quite differently from modern systems. Instead of beginning with an elaborate section on footwork and guards to stand in, or long solo drills designed to help you memorize a wide number of techniques, similar to learning your ABCs when we begin to learn to read and write, I argue that Liechtenauer and his successors began by teaching their students a single strike, the *Zornhau*, and a small number of permutations. Then, after an extended section developing general fighting skills with these techniques, they introduced the other four strikes of their system and their permutations. On the way through the five strikes Ringeck briefly introduces the students to virtually all of the 'advanced' techniques, the guards, and explains how to attack, counter, prevent, or avoid these 'advanced' moves with the five strikes and their permutations. Ringeck does not address how to execute these 'advanced' techniques or even how to use the guards until later in the curriculum.

The masters of the Liechtenauer tradition almost always describe their methods and techniques in the form of partner drills, very similar to the methods of other ancient swordsmanship styles from many other parts of the world. This methodology often relies on the assumption that there is a person teaching the art who knows what they're doing, understands what the student needs to learn, who will not fall into bad habits, and who has the perspective to embody and explain each principle and technique to their students. I believe that this methodology provides a simple curriculum, meant to train someone to fight for their life very quickly, in a matter of weeks, if not days.[11]

I claim that the *Zornhau* section was specifically designed to teach, with a single general-purpose strike, how to counter virtually all potential techniques, and thus prepare someone to fight quickly. It is, I claim, a sort of miniature fighting style all on its own, a microcosm of the larger *Kunst des Fechtens*, and, therefore, the perfect introduction to the larger style, because it can operate independently, and mesh readily with the later techniques. When my students finish the *Zornhau* section, and its supplementary material, I have them take their first rank test. This usually takes at least six months.

I believe that Liechtenauer and his students intended that their art would be learned step by step in the order they laid out, possibly even spending several practice sessions learning and ingraining each technique in their students before progressing on, as each step lays groundwork necessary for understanding the next one. This makes a strict class lesson plan in the modern sense, where the dates and times for particular lessons are set in advance, unhelpful. Doing this interrupts the natural flow of learning each student moves through. It expands their minds to the eventual possibilities, but it delays their mastery of the fundamental skills.

To this end, a teacher of this art should keep themselves deeply aware of the progress of each of their students. By understanding where they stand on the path to mastery a teacher should be able to guide each of them as they move along to the next step. At the core of this path are the partner drills. Each drill needs its own specific approach phase and sequence of permutations to ensure that the students learn correct measure, timing, priority, courage, and form. The student learns to feel from each bind how best to exploit the opponent's openings, while sensing which opening the opponent will aim for and how to attack with the very same motion that they will use to defend themselves. Throughout this process the teacher must ensure that the student understands what they aim to learn in each and every exchange.

Periodically, Ringeck writes that a student should learn to find ways to act on their own, or specifically allow for other unlisted permutations, encouraging creativity. I interpret these sections as excellent places to introduce sparring, and I spend several sessions doing a lot of it, emphasizing inclusion of the techniques they have been learning. Sparring should be done with the specific intent of teaching the students the instincts for the creative flexibility necessary for a successful martial artist, and to test how well they have ingrained their training. Sparring also works well to teach courage, timing, targeting, and working under pressure.

Building skill through drills, however, seems to be the chief concern of the Liechtenauer tradition's teachings, and that of virtually all other historical European martial arts of which we have record. Partner drills, and not sparring, solo drills, or test cutting, serve as the best method of building skill. Three capacities comprise skill: the ability to choose the correct technique for a given situation, the capacity to execute the technique correctly, and the capacity to gauge at what specific moment to execute it. Sparring does not increase one's ability to choose the correct technique for a given situation, or the ability to execute it correctly, though it can help you improve your timing for those techniques. Sparring can, however, test how far one has come in all three aspects of skill. Only through isolation and abstraction can one focus on a particular element of skill clearly enough to improve it, and that requires tightly controlled partner drills.

It is also important that a student spar with unfamiliar and unfriendly opponents. You should visit other schools, attend major events, and participate in tournaments, ideally with your whole group. Once a student has mastered the *Zornhau* section, which this book is designed to encompass, they will have a complete, if simple, technique set, and it is appropriate for them to begin sparring regularly, and to compete, if they so desire. If, however, a student's technique breaks down under the pressures of sparring they need to return to the drills, executing them with more vigor, intent, and variations of speed to learn their lessons until they become instinctive.

How then shall we describe our ideal fighter produced by training in this style? A thoroughly trained fighter of the Liechtenauer tradition calmly perceives their opponents' threats and openings clearly, in spite of attempts at deception and distraction. They choose their attack and proceed swiftly and confidently at the target without wasting time or motion. Their attacks use correct form, measure, timing, and body mechanics to force the opponent to meet them in very specific ways. They never let their opponent have the breathing room they need to pursue their own offenses. The constant threats the Liechtenauer fighter poses punish their opponents' mistakes, and each of those same motions cover the targets threatened by their opponent. They use their strength, quickness, perception, feeling, thoroughly trained technique, and courage to walk right into their opponent's space and beat them. When they find themselves needing to make a defense, they will defend in ways that simultaneously attack, forcing the opponent to return to the pattern above.

Among advanced practitioners this might look on the surface like the standard attack > parry > riposte > parry > riposte fighting of many systems, but nothing could be further from the truth. Many systems rely on clearly separated attacks and defenses. Virtually all of their techniques are executed and taught in a sequence that treats them separately. Their defenses buy them time with which they can make their attacks. Liechtenauer's system, on the other hand, integrates the defensive and offensive elements together, with the notable exception of the *Krumphau Absetzen*, which I hope to deal with in another volume. Liechtenauer's Five Strikes offer the potential to fight this way, and other strikes do not offer the same opportunities. Most students easily grasp the offensive mindset, but it often takes a lot of training to join defenses to the attacks in a burgeoning fighter's technique. Between two ideal practitioners of this style there are only the smallest of margins for error, and the first person to make a mistake should be instantly struck.

I want to further explain a unique characteristic of Ringeck's teaching style: he introduces the guards, and most of the 'advanced' techniques and counters relatively early on, but he seems to do so only to expose the students to them, not to teach them how to use them. These early lessons serve as preventative measures to avoid leaving his students vulnerable. The 'advanced' techniques, such as *Durchwechseln*, *Uberlauffen* and *Nachreissen*, are often dealt with obliquely, but you can find within Ringeck's early advice information crucial to avoid leaving oneself open to these techniques. Do not let these brief exposures become their own lessons while the student is still learning their foundational skill set.

Chapter 3

Interpretation

Interpreting ancient manuals can be quite difficult. There are five major steps to develop a successful interpretation. To a certain extent all HEMA practitioners will need to do this for themselves, even if they have a competent teacher and a more or less complete text. I've tried to design this book to do most of the hard work for you, but you should be aware of the process as you'll most likely have to do some of it yourself. My goal is, and has always been, not just to re-create the techniques, but the way they were taught, because I believe that methodology and pedagogy shape the lessons learned.

1. Interpret

Hypothesize how a technique is executed. Pay careful attention to the text, if there are illustrations cross-reference the ones in the source you are working from with contemporary works, then test the idea out in a practical sense with training swords, and protective gear. Protective gear is often necessary for interpretive work because you are not training, you are guessing and testing. Using force and intent to achieve a realistic impact is absolutely necessary to develop a good hypothesis. You will often go through numerous iterations as you refine your hypothesis. It is very important that you take the whole corpus of a manual into account. Try to stick as closely to that as possible when you do this. Also be careful of changes that protective gear introduces. After you have a sound idea of its execution remove the protective gear and, relying on control, test the technique more.

2. Drilling

Once you have a working interpretation you need to come up with a drill to learn the technique, so you can repeat it over and over until you can do it instinctively. Remember to always include the approach phase to ingrain control of the distance of the fight, and a withdrawal phase to keep your mind in the fight until you reach a safe distance. The language of the manual you've chosen should guide you here. You will often need to return to this stage when you encounter problems making the techniques work. Sometimes you will have interpreted the material incorrectly. Sometimes there are subtleties of body mechanics that you have overlooked. Most of the time, you will find that you simply haven't drilled enough. Pay special attention to the manual, the iconography, and what can be gleaned from surviving martial arts in terms of both similarities and differences to create these methods, drills, and forms.

3. Sparring

You must then attempt to use your technique in an unstructured scenario. Preferably against opponents that you are unfamiliar with, while accounting for the unrealistic aspects of what you are doing. If it works as it is supposed to, accounting for safety measures and differences in the weapons used from historical precedent, and realism versus the abstraction of sparring, and so on, then if you are defeated by the proper counters, and win when you exploit the advantages indicated in the manual, you can take that as evidence that you have, generally speaking, interpreted the technique correctly. Always seek to refine your interpretation by finding new insights, evidence, and permutations, and understand your defeats as opportunities to find these. Unlike drills, in these bouts creative thinking and variation should be encouraged. Constantly seek new opponents and new opportunities to test your ideas.

I strongly recommend that all HEMA practitioners read Mike Edelson's article: 'Western Martial Arts Bouting: Recognizing and Dealing with Artifacts in Free Play'. It offers the most thorough treatment of the subject of problems that crop up in sparring, and bad habits that can be developed, how to watch for them, how to avoid them, and how to fix them. To quote him: 'you should take great care to treat the sword, whether it is blunt steel, or a padded simulator, as though it were the real thing. If someone is treating it like a game, stop and explain why this is wrong, and if he or she continues to fight with reset button mentality, find someone else to train with.'

4. Test cutting

After you have verified your interpretation you must do physical testing to learn how the cuts, slices, and thrusts work, and to see if what you are doing would work in reality. With longswords, this should primarily take the form of test cutting. I strongly recommend soaked tatami mats. While there is little direct evidence of test cutting of any kind being a historical practice in the Middle Ages and the Renaissance, there are examples from Europe in later periods. I, and many others, find test cutting incredibly valuable for verifying theories and finding flaws in cutting technique. You should work with a real sword as much as possible. Having access to a well-made sword with a design based on rigorous historical research is essential for a successful group.[12]

Two points to note about needing a sharp sword to train with. First, when you're cutting correctly your sword should make a whistle that is long, clear, and sharp. Listen for it. You should hear it every time you swing. If you do not, practice more. Second, while outside the scope of the techniques in this volume, it is impossible to learn half-swording techniques properly without a sharp sword. Many of the manuals that show half-swording in unarmored combat show it done with sharp swords and bare hands. Hopefully you will have built up some significant calluses from your training by the time you start learning these techniques. It bears the danger of minor cuts to your hands, but learning how to grip a sharp sword safely and strike without cutting yourself, simply cannot be done with a blunt.

5. Get more perspectives

You should then compare your interpretation with other people working on the same material and with similar martial arts. This will often bring things to your attention that you hadn't thought of before. Sometimes you will find distinctions or similarities between the different martial arts styles or interpretations. Besides these valuable benefits, cross-training with other groups is exceptionally fun and important for spreading knowledge about historical European martial arts. From here you can repeat the process with your newfound knowledge.

Chapter 4

Safety

Martial arts distill violence into a concentrated form. They pose inherent danger, especially when practiced correctly. The whole point of a martial art is to learn how you might neutralize a threat to the life or liberty of yourself or another person by using force. Training in martial arts is fraught with minor bumps and bruises as well as the occasional injury of a more serious nature, such as broken bones or bad sprains, and there just isn't any way around it. Nevertheless, even reconstructed martial arts can be learned in a way that is historically accurate and does not risk death or permanent injury.

Evidence for ancient training methods of warriors in Europe can only be had piecemeal, and really merits its own volume, but I'll endeavor to condense the conclusions of historical research and archaeological findings on the methods of training in historical European swordsmanship here. Bear in mind many styles may have used only some of these, and that all of these were also done mounted as well as on foot.[13]

- Partner drills with real weapons without protective gear, or with only gloves
- Partner drills with training weapons without protective gear, or only gloves
- Partner drills in armor
- Solo exercises with a weapon or training weapon
- Striking a pell, or similar target, with a real or training weapon
- Competing in tournaments both with and without armor
- Sparring
- Challenging other swordsmen to both friendly, and sometimes not so friendly, combat
- Calisthenics and tumbling
- Calisthenics and tumbling in armor
- Weight training
- Wrestling
- Hunting
- Riding, racing, and equestrian sports

The vast majority of material from surviving manuals on unarmored fencing depicts the first two kinds of practice. I believe that paired drills without protective gear, beyond the occasional set of gloves, which, incidentally, show up in surprisingly few manuals, formed the core of their training regimen and that they devoted the bulk of their training time to it. While I believe that training with real swords in carefully choreographed drills was probably done, I also believe it was reserved for advanced students with thousands of hours of hard training under their belt. I further believe that paired drills with training weapons and little or no protective gear should constitute the vast majority of modern training regimens.

Some people might object to my assessment of the historical training methodologies because it does not match modern sensibilities or conventions. Many modern groups wear a great deal of safety gear throughout virtually all their training. I believe we should train the way our historical predecessors did for purposes of historicity, to maintain a focused and serious mindset in our classes, to foster the development of skill, and, though it might sound strange to some people, because I have found that it is safer than the alternatives.

When we look at ancient sources from all over the world depicting warriors training for unarmored combat, we do not see much safety gear. When we look at the old martial arts that have survived to this day, we do not see safety gear unless it was introduced in the last few hundred years, well after close combat arts began to seriously decline in usefulness in military contexts, and well after the line between martial art and martial sport began to blur. In ancient sources we see warriors with training swords, or real swords. We do not see them wearing helmets, armor, gauntlets, padding, or any such thing when practicing unarmored combat, though they often would have possessed such gear for participating in tournaments and warfare. Indeed, only when they are explicitly training for armored combat or participating in tournaments do we consistently see them wear protective gear at all.[14]

When we look at the evidence of the ancient sword arts that have survived from before 1600, the various koryu styles from Japan, sword styles from China's Ming period, Indian and Pakistani styles, and others, we see that they did not use much in the way of safety equipment when training for unarmored combat either. Some of them even train extensively with sharp swords to this day. In point of fact, I have never seen a manual, tapestry, or painting from anywhere in medieval or Renaissance Europe depicting ancient warriors practicing unarmored techniques with more protective gear than a pair of gloves. Training armor comparable to our modern training armor for unarmored fighting did exist, but it cannot have been commonplace if the frequency of surviving evidence both written and archaeological is anything to go on.

The training armor used in modern kendo wasn't invented until almost 1700, nearly a century into the relatively peaceful Edo period.[15] In Europe, while some precursors have been found, the fencing mask's invention and broad acceptance only occurred at the end of the eighteenth century, long after the sword had lost its place among the primary weapons of war, and learning swordsmanship served mainly as a form of sport, and, to a lesser extent, self-defense, or for duels of honor.[16] Dueling had already become less common among dwindling classes of noblemen, and the manuals on the use of the sword in war during that time show considerable simplification, due to needing to be taught to massive numbers of soldiers rather than elite cadres of warriors.[17]

Why should martial arts have been taught this way for so many centuries and in so many places before the modern era? Why didn't lethal or maiming training accidents beset all of these warrior cultures so badly that they adopted lots of training armor? Why was this the case in so many different places, times, and among so many cultures? Why did this not change until well into periods when swords ceased to be major components of most military fighting? After a lot of cuts, bumps, and bruises, I have come to the conclusion that the most likely reason they did this is because what keeps a person safe in training isn't actually the safety equipment they use, but the discipline of one's training partner. In my experience no amount of safety equipment can remove the possibility of minor or even serious injuries. In fact, all of the serious injuries I have seen or read about in martial arts training happened because one of the persons involved ignored protocol, lost control, or attempted something beyond their skill level.

I repeat: no protective gear can totally remove the possibility of serious injury from martial arts training. If your training partner executes a technique of distilled violence against you without restraint, then he or she risks doing you serious harm, no matter the protective gear you've acquired. In my experience strictly teaching and expecting control and responsible behavior removes the threat of injury far more effectively than relying on protective gear. In a day and age when medical techniques and technology were unreliable at best, and when many of their students were powerful and influential people, preserving the safety of the students in training would have been of even more importance then than it is today.

Now I do believe training armor can be useful. They can use it to practice making their strikes and thrusts with force and intent, especially when targeting sensitive areas. It also provides essential protection for tournament settings where high levels of control should not be expected. Even then, a student cannot afford to totally abandon control lest they risk seriously injuring their opponent. Historical European methods for gaining the experience such practice delivers were largely limited to armored fighting in armored and unarmored tournaments, and pell training. Medieval tournaments were fraught with injuries, and the occasional death, in spite of the fact that much of their safety equipment was as good as, or in some cases superior to, modern equipment.

Ancient European warriors usually owned their own weapons and armor. They might possess helmets, gauntlets, breastplates, greaves, and a lot of other equipment, only a fraction of which is required by most modern HEMA schools. They were also often better made, better designed, and better fitted than the vast majority of the equipment that most modern practitioners use. So why do the images in the manuals they wrote not show them they constantly using them in practice to improve the safety of their training?

First, wearing protective gear changes the way you can move, it changes how you can see, it adds extra weight, restricts your flexibility and reach, and of necessity changes the way you think about your movements. On top of that it does that to your opponent as well, so that they will act somewhat differently than an unarmored opponent. When training for armored combat this becomes absolutely necessary, and most manuals with sections on armored combat depict their subjects wearing armor for their training, because you need to be prepared to deal with those changes when you fight in armor. When training for unarmored combat, however, all the manuals from this period that I have examined myself depict people wearing their normal clothing and no protective gear.

Second, since safety cannot be perfectly achieved by the addition of protective gear, but can be by learning control, protective gear is ultimately unnecessary during normal training. I believe historical warriors learned a far greater degree of control, and the mechanics of their techniques to a much higher degree of perfection, than most modern groups do, and this, more than anything else, kept them safe. Now for unfriendly sparring matches and tournaments we do find examples of protective gear being used, but just as often we find historical examples of these being fought with training weapons or even real weapons without serious injuries.

The most common response I encounter to this evidence is that ancient peoples had different notions of safety and different expectations of normal training injuries. There is something to this in their competition rule sets, but for training the objection seems largely baseless. The lack of evidence of training injuries and the extremely refined quality of European armor is a testament to their concern for safety during dangerous activities. Their armorers came from traditions hundreds of years old, with tens of thousands of real battlefield tests to draw knowledge from. They could have worn their armor in training, but they seem only to have done so when they were training for armored combat. Moreover, medicine in the time period was far less reliable than it is today, and this greater risk of complications from injuries would have informed their training practices.

Now, I'd like to briefly turn our attention to the aforementioned chief exception among their training exercises to the method I'm suggesting, the tournament. European warriors regarded these events as an integral part of their training, and here we would see armored warriors, sometimes wearing armor specifically designed for tournaments, which is exactly the opposite of the training method I advocate should make up the majority of our work. This also serves as evidence that they trained in such armor in preparation for tournaments. It also means that they must have spent some time training with the limited technique sets designed for tournaments. The serious accidents that happened in ancient tournaments should make us cautious about using period correct rule sets and equipment as a regular part of everyday practice.

Ideally, we should follow in their footsteps in taking part in tournaments, and try to use their rule sets and conventions as starting points for our own modern practices. Some of the techniques in the Liechtenauer tradition would have been illegal in some of tournaments of the era. So, it's clear that the warriors of the period understood the difference between training for tournaments, and training for real combat in a profound way. I argue that tournament fighting, and preparation, serves as the exception that proves the rule, not the other way around.

Below I will outline my methods for making training safe:

- Use properly made training swords for partner training. These training tools can seriously hurt your training partner if you do not use control, and you will know immediately when you start to exceed your limits. Also, high quality equipment is less prone to breaking, which often produces unforeseen actions, and can leave sharp points which one might not notice quickly enough to prevent an accident.
- Begin slowly enough to be able to stop your blade at or just before contact without fail. Do not tolerate accidents: they are symptomatic of poor preparation and control. Slowly build up your control until you can work at high speeds while making gentle contact or demonstrating that you could make contact without touching your opponent. Expect this to take a few weeks.
- With a longsword, the sword hand (the one near the crossguard) should be guiding the blade and using an appropriate striking motion, which will be covered in detail in the section on cutting. You can alter the speed of your strike with the motion of this hand, and this will chiefly determine how hard you will hit your opponent. The off hand, however, controls the blade's extension in the cut and the forward snapping motion of the blade. It plays a crucial role in developing power in a real fight, but it also provides a mechanism for positioning the weapon properly without hurting your training partner when you are practicing, especially in unexpected situations. You can conveniently arrest your blade's motion with your off hand by simply resisting the primary motion. Thrusts are best controlled with careful knowledge of the distance at which you are thrusting and sensitive flexibility in your arms.
- High-intensity sparring with tournament-level safety gear, especially helmets, and hand protection, is necessary for perfecting intent and testing one's growth. Joint protection for the elbows and knees, protection for the groin, and shin

guards are also advisable for this kind of activity. I should note, however, that hard sparring does not justify throwing your control out the window. You must maintain a high level of control, even when sparring this way, to avoid injury, even if you are allowing hard hits, and have adequate protection.

- Simultaneously, you should train in solo drills with the intent of learning to cut and thrust as if actually striking an opponent. Ideally you should go through the full motions with a real weapon. When you cut with a real sword properly you should hear a nice, long, sharp whistle as you cut through the air. You should also train with a pell, an old tree, or another person holding targets so that you can perfect your targeting and grasp of measure with strong contact.
- You should regularly do test cutting a few times a year. There is no hard evidence of test cutting in medieval or Renaissance Europe, though there is some record of early modern cavalrymen from eastern Europe cutting clay mixed with straw.[18] Nevertheless, our modern situation makes it necessary that we gain practical experience cutting. It is amazing to me how many students can spar pretty well, but cannot cut worth beans. The Japanese practice of cutting tatami mats is, I believe, the best such training method available to us.
- You should also try to experience the competitive side of training through in-house competition, and by attending regional tournaments.

The end result should be regular practices that look a lot more like old-school Japanese *koryu* training, with lots of high-speed drilling, and a lot less like a contemporary HEMA tournament. Frankly, I believe that something like this is what most ancient masters, and Ringeck in particular, did. Practice your drills with as much realism, speed, and intent as you can safely muster. When done properly, every one of these drills should push us as hard as any other training method. If you let your group's drills become empty forms, then you have failed your group. If you let people use relaxed slow drills for purposes other than to establish correct form, you are failing to use them correctly. Make sparring and tournaments the exceptions that prove the rule in your club.

Some might object that this can impede a student's ability to strike with intent. This is a potential problem. I have had some students with whom I had to work on this issue. In my experience, however, it is far easier to get a student to loosen their control than to tighten it up.

How does this work in terms of safety? My self-control first training method has a pretty good track record. I've been teaching using this method for more than a decade. My group regularly has a very few minor bumps and bruises. They consistently throw each other to the ground, and we must deal with the aches and pains that come with that, but none of them have lost an eye or a finger. None of them has had a training partner break the bones of their fingers, hands, wrist, neck or back. None of them has had a concussion. In the years I've been instructing people in historical European martial arts with this safety method only one of my students has had a serious injury. A young man at one of the summer camps for high-schoolers I ran back in 2009 broke his toe from poor stepping. Nevertheless, he came back the next day with his foot in a brace and cheerfully participated in every training activity. I'd also like to emphasize that this injury did not come from a lack of a training partner's control. On the other hand, the groups I've observed who rely chiefly on protective gear to keep them safe typically neglect the serious control training I advocate, and in my experience they have far more injuries than my group.

So that's the way I train. It's the way I think historical warriors trained. I think it's the fastest, safest, most historically accurate way to train historical European martial arts. I strongly urge you to try training this way, for your own safety.

Chapter 5

Sparring

Sparring, along with interpretation, drills, and test cutting, makes up one of the most crucial parts of learning historical European martial arts. It is something that every martial artist should do regularly.

Once you have mastered the execution of your technique set nearly every training session should contain some sparring. It serves as one of the best tests of how well you have learned the art you have set out to learn, and how successful your interpretation is. If you can keep your cool, see the situations as they develop naturally, choose the correct techniques, and apply them in their intended contexts, then you know your training is paying off. If, when you execute techniques in sparring, you end up making them work the way the manual tells you they should, then you will know that you have made real progress. Sparring will tell you if you have learned your techniques correctly, because you will be able to apply them under pressure from an opponent who resists you. Sparring can teach you to apply the knowledge of distance, timing, courage, strategy, initiative, and footwork perhaps better than any other training method. Sparring also tests your creativity and capacity to apply techniques in the odd situations that invariably crop up.

Sparring can also become counterproductive, especially in swordplay. I have learned through hard experience that it takes a great deal of practice and drilling to apply techniques properly in hard sparring, and that sparring before that training has sunk in can actually impede a fighter's ability to learn to apply a technique. Because of this, I will make a fairly radical claim. Sparring by advanced students should look choreographed most of the time because they will have, in fact, practiced each technique and variation 20,000 times. I claim that if your sparring doesn't look largely like your technique training then either you have not truly mastered your techniques, or your technique training is unrealistic, and has gaps that need to be filled.

Some groups use success in sparring as the supreme measure of skill. In my view sparring cannot be the ultimate test of skill, or an interpretation for that matter. Nor should it be the end in and of itself. Sparring can only serve to offer part of a complete training experience. It serves best as a regular exercise for experienced students, and as a method of testing an interpretation. Sparring isn't fighting, and sparring weapons aren't real weapons. The results of a sparring match do not always indicate the results of a real fight between the fighters. I estimate that at least 20% of sparring matches would progress differently if they were done for real. You can, however, use sparring to learn timing, application of leverage, feeling, control, courage, creative use of techniques, and how to seize the *Vor*. Sometimes when used to test interpretations the method of sparring should be quite different from a normal sparring match. Because each technique is designed for a particular situation, sometimes testing an interpretation requires a limited form of sparring where one or both opponents must begin in a set guard, or with a particular technique, and sometimes with a designated initial attacker and defender. I've employed numerous such activities in my teaching, usually as the capstones of particular sections.

I also wish to emphasize that cutting technique, which is essential to good strikes, cannot be learned or tested in sparring. It is learned by swinging a real sword and listening for the whistle which the blade makes. It is tested by attempting to cut targets that are properly resistant, such as pork, clothing, and tatami mats. Some people I have met are excellent in sparring and deficient in cutting technique, which means that if they were to attempt to fight for real with a sword it is very possible that a blow of theirs which would look clean in sparring would do comparatively little damage in a real fight. I believe that ancient warriors probably learned good cutting technique to a high level, and probably before they did a great deal of sparring.

Intensive drills, and not sparring, offer the best way to learn techniques. When done with proper intent and speed, they should present just as much of a challenge as a sparring match. In fact, I believe that the line between drills and sparring should become very thin as you progress through the teachings of Ringeck and Liechtenauer. Drills build skills, and sparring tests them.

For the above reasons I believe that a serious student should not engage in sparring for fun or sport until they can employ a complete set of techniques competently. This doesn't mean you have to wait until you have finished an a multi-year training program, but in Ringeck's style, for example, a student should have at least been introduced to the foundational teachings in the *Zornhau* section so that they can have a response to virtually any attack before they begin sparring. They should be at this point by the end of the curriculum in this volume. If you begin to spar a lot before you have learned your techniques properly you will develop bad habits that must be unlearned before you can continue to improve.

If people spar without respect for the weapon, if they accept double hits and after-blows in order to get hits in, then there is something wrong with their mindset about their sparring, and you need to tell them so. In a tournament setting one could argue that winning could be a primary goal, but it should never become the only goal. We must always strive toward our larger goals of learning historical arts accurately, being realistic in our re-creations of them, and keeping our training partners and ourselves safe. In class, winning must be a secondary goal to these other goals. You must see yourself first as a student, learning the things that sparring teaches. Focusing on winning at the expense of learning leads to injuries, and the adoption of bad habits. Sparring requires absolute honesty about your art, intentions, and what happened in each and every match. The only place where winning should be the chief goal pursued at the expense of all others is in a real fight. The value of sparring also changes a great deal depending on the context and rule set employed. Most sparring is simply done one-on-one, with similar weapons, to the first 'good' hit, in a manner which most closely approximates an unarmored duel. Sparring can, however, simulate asymmetric situations with different weapons, different numbers of opponents on each side, and different starting situations, such as sitting down, being attacked from behind, having your weapon sheathed, or simply emphasizing different target areas, and so on. One popular historical tournament rule set from the period I study - and let me note that I actually prefer this to the standard method of fighting until the first hit is scored - was to fight until a set number of attacks had been attempted, and the person who struck the best blow in the course of the bout was declared the winner. This teaches persistence, respect for the threats of second and third actions, and prepares a student psychologically to stay in the fight longer. Like all sparring methods it has pros and cons, but I find it very valuable as a training method, and the fact that it was done in Ringeck's time is a strong point in its favor. Varying sparring rules makes your sparring much more informative, and more fun.

Sparring, unlike drills, should always include some safety equipment. You should at least use a good helmet and hand protection. If you can get more protection for your throat, elbows, and knees, this can be very helpful as well. A gambeson will reduce the number of bruises you receive. Remember, the chief point of safety equipment should not be to make the experience more comfortable, but to prevent accidents from causing serious injury. Remember, also no amount of safety gear can totally remove the need for control.

Chapter 6

Martial Arts and Martial Sports

Most people do not understand that there is a difference between martial arts and martial sports or why that difference matters. Sometimes students even have a hard time identifying which they are practicing. The difference matters a great deal. The nature of your art or sport ties you to its purposes and function. When people ask me 'What's the difference between a martial art and a martial sport?' I answer that a martial art prepares you to fight for real, while a martial sport prepares you to fight in a special sport context and can teach some very specific things about fighting that are impossible to learn any other way. Each fulfill different purposes, and serious students of either should practice both, as most European warriors historically did.

Martial arts are systems of fighting designed to defeat an opponent who intends to injure, capture, or kill you. They achieve their goal if you successfully defend yourself, your liberty, your country and your loved ones; or if you chase off a foe, force them to surrender, give them an incapacitating injury, render them unconscious, create space for you to escape, capture an opponent, or, particularly in arts that involve weapons, kill your foe. Martial arts may be trained and applied anywhere; the terrain may affect the tactical decisions you make, and escape is often an option, or even the chief objective. Martial arts also usually spend some time dealing with how to fight multiple opponents. Martial arts usually expose their students to a very wide set of contexts in which to apply their technique. Martial arts use equipment both in the abstract to learn certain skills, as well as to prepare for practical application, and martial arts practitioners frequently handle real weapons. Martial artists train from the ground up in techniques and thinking that cannot be had in martial sports.

Martial sports, on the other hand, are designed to defeat an opponent who wishes to best you in a contest, often with some risk, or even guarantee, of physical injury. The goal in a martial sport is to win by scoring points, obtaining a submission hold, or rendering an opponent unconscious. Serious injuries can happen, but they usually happen by accident, or at least without intention, and most commonly when an opponent deliberately chooses to violate the rules and spirit of the contest. Martial sports are almost always conducted in a special arena from which escape is impossible, and which has as little effect on the internal tactical options of the contest as possible. The equipment in martial sports is almost always designed to be precisely similar and to avoid serious injury.

Martial sports allow several unique experiences that are valuable for self-improvement and self-defense, and some of these cannot be had any other way. They allow you to face an unfamiliar opponent determined to beat you, usually without serious physical danger, but not often without pain, and in a manner that can be repeated and refined. Martial sports should be used to learn courage, timing, measure, judgment, how to read an opponent, and how to perform under pressure.

To some extent martial arts and martial sports are different species of activities, and never the twain shall meet, but I believe that one can, and should, follow the historical precedent of the European traditions and participate in both martial arts and martial sports to take advantage of those exclusive experiences. People can only do this profitably when they understand the differences, distinctions, and common pitfalls in these two very different activities.

On the surface the distinctions between martial arts and martial sports can seem blurry to outsiders, such as when one observes judo practitioners and koryu practitioners doing grappling techniques. In these cases, the chief differences in many of the techniques come from the mindset and contexts in which they design and apply their techniques, or in their mode of presentation. In fact many martial arts, such as Muay Thai, Karate, and Tae Kwon Do, have martial sports that specifically and intentionally parallel them, and are practiced as a necessary and integral element of their martial arts training. Sometimes they even share the same name and school and may therefore be referred to as either completely accurately and blur the line considerably.

The differences in the moves and among the move-sets do not often matter all that much when practitioners spar with each other in friendly matches. To an outsider when you pit a fighter from a martial sport and a fighter from a martial art with the same roots together for a friendly sparring match, the two will seem to be doing similar things. They will understand each other's movements, they will use similar tactics, and the results will look similar no matter which one wins, especially if the match's rules forbid permanently damaging their opponent. If, on the other hand, you pair them off against an opponent with a knife, gun, club, or sword, or an opponent who knows how to injure them with their bare hands and is willing, or even eager, to do so, or set them against multiple opponents, or in difficult terrain, the differences will become apparent.

Sometimes these differences can be quite stark, such as when one contrasts modern sport fencing with historical European swordsmanship. Sport fencing takes place on a narrow strip which the participants may not leave, while in historical swordsmanship the place for practice or combat is selected for strategic considerations, proximity, or convenience, and the footwork possible may be very different. In some settings, like duels, this would be an open field, or an arena with a great deal of flat space on either side of the combatants, but training and combat may also take place in a setting with terrain obstructing the combatants, and the combatants may move around it however they like such as on a narrow bridge or in a thick forest, on horseback, in a room filled with tables and chairs, or on a ladder going up a wall. In sport fencing the weaponry used resembles real weapons only in the most superficial ways. It does not weigh or behave at all like the weapons they are simulating, and in their practice sport fencers typically pay very little attention to these differences. Very importantly, winners are always declared.

In historical swordsmanship you are either training with real weapons or with tools that simulate real weapons as closely as possible, or at least in certain specific ways appropriate to the training method you are employing. Understanding the differences between your training tools and real weapons must be part and parcel of the practice. When you spar, you spar to prove your interpretation, test your learning, and have fun in the process, and you should evaluate each match based on what the real world results should have been, regardless of whether the rules say you should have scored more or fewer points, and we must acknowledge situations where both participants will have been wounded or killed.

In sport fencing participants must respect a very specific set of rules including: right of way, prohibitions on grappling, stepping off of the lane the competition takes place on, grabbing their opponent's weapon, and so on. There are some sets of ancient tournament rules that use somewhat similar restrictions, but they also differ in important ways, and in the way they were enforced. I also wish to point out that these precedents are evidence from historical martial sports, which directly paralleled historical martial arts as a subset of larger training regimens, but were not, in and of themselves, martial arts. Modern analysis of bodies in ancient battle graves and writings on ancient swordsmanship clearly indicate that while the target locations incentivized by such rule-sets often reflect reality, and were usually considered preferable, no such restrictions were absolute when it came to maiming and killing real people.[19]

One classic example of the difference between martial arts and martial sports which can be readily seen online comes from the show *Human Weapon* in its Krav Maga episode. Watch the first knife training sequences. You will see these trained fighters, who often excel in the ring, struggle to intuitively comprehend and adjust to the physical realities of facing a weapon, until after they are taught how to do so. I have seen exactly the same thing happen when I teach someone who has learned a martial sport, often believing it was a martial art, but which did not even teach how to deal with an opponent with a knife, the most basic of all weapons. They see an opening which would be safe to attack if they were fighting an unarmed opponent, their instincts kick in, and they attack. I've even seen some needlessly discard their own weapons to do a move they know well, but which requires two hands. They almost always succeed in applying their technique, only to find out that the relatively gentle poking they are feeling on their head, neck, back, chest, or side, would probably have killed them in a real fight.

This I think best demonstrates how martial arts and martial sports differ. Martial sports prioritize their movements according to the points they would score, the positions they would obtain, or knockouts they would achieve. Some of these would work well in a real fight, some wouldn't, and martial sports fighters are, unfortunately, sometimes completely ignorant of which they should and shouldn't use in a situation where the goal is self-defense. Some mistakes I frequently see include: disregarding a dangerous weapon in order to execute a 'winning' technique, intentionally going to the ground with their opponent when there are multiple opponents or weapons that can hit them up close, and doing techniques which would leave them open to eye gouges, bone breaks, and other potentially maiming techniques which are not allowed in their sport's rule-sets.

Now I do not mean to say that people who practice martial sports cannot defend themselves. Many practitioners of martial sports are indeed fearsome fighters. Many would be superior to me, and many other martial artists, in many contexts, as seen by the many instances in which martial sport practitioners have beaten attackers in self-defense, and martial artists in challenges. Many of them have also taken the time to learn how to deal with the specific situations outside the purview of their sports. I applaud those who have reached such high accomplishments, and I believe that those accomplishments are worthwhile in and of themselves.

Let me stress again that I believe that practicing martial sports is necessary to becoming a good martial artist. Martial sports have their problems, tournaments are inherently flawed, the contexts are unrealistic, and the prioritizing of techniques has to be adjusted for a real fight, but only in a martial sport can one practice against an opponent who is both unfamiliar and eager to beat you. They provide one of the best ways to test yourself and your training. Having said that, I believe that a person who desires to be a successful martial artist will have to be vigilant to ensure that they do not become involved in the worst aspects of martial sport competition: gaming the system, failing to adjust their technique in other contexts, losing perspective of the context, lack of control, and worst of all, arrogance bred from winning too much, or discouragement from winning too little. I argue that while it can be difficult to avoid these things, martial sports come from historical precedents for good reasons, and I participate in them every chance I get, and I encourage my students to do likewise.

The modern HEMA tournament scene is still new. Right now, we have many different rule-sets, equipment requirements, and procedures, but a lot of forces are pushing for standardization, in an attempt to reach for the highest possible standard. I believe that while this has been the right path to take so far, that no single rule set is sufficient in and of itself to serve as the perfect parallel for the fighting arts we practice, nor should such rule-sets, however well-conceived, serve as a general guide to our martial arts training. I argue that our tournament rule-sets should become more diverse as the years go on. Using many different rule-sets will help ensure that we remember that tournaments are an abstraction. It will also make it much harder to game the system, because there will be many systems, not just one.

Ancient warriors conducted competitions in their schools, towns, countries, and even internationally. Such competition helped produce effective warriors, gave them experience against people of other styles, and served as advertising for their skills and services. Modern competition can and should serve the same functions. It helps build courage, the capacity to work and think under pressure, creativity, mental flexibility, and a fighting spirit. It also lets people have a fairly good idea of who is better than whom, with probably up to around 80% accuracy. Participating in martial sports follows historical precedent, and I argue it must have a place in the work of a dedicated martial artist. So, get out there and compete.

Chapter 7

Defining Ringeck's Weapon

Masters of the Liechtenauer tradition called the weapon used in their art the *langeschwert* or 'longsword' in English. The words longsword, bastard sword, war sword, and two-hand sword, were all used historically to describe types of swords used in this tradition. 'Longsword,' however, is the term which Liechtenauer and Ringeck used, so I suggest your group use the term 'longsword.'

Oakeshott's typology of medieval swords recognizes approximately twelve major varieties of longsword, with a number of sub-varieties. Later scholars have complicated this typology with other observations. For the purposes of learning how to use these weapons, however, such a classification system offers nothing informative. Which is to say, that the same set of techniques can be done with most such weapons. Their differences in size, shape, cross-section, or the form of their hilt, grip, or pommel make little difference to the techniques that can be done with them. These older weapon typologies do not tell us how well these swords do these different things, or which techniques and fighting styles they favor. Different kinds of longswords excel at different portions of the broader technique set they all share, but they all share the same technique set. Early war swords of the late medieval period, and some large Renaissance longswords with cutting oriented blades, such as those featured in the Goliath manual, favor the initial cut at long range. Shorter thrusting oriented bastard swords, on the other hand, such as the swords seen in Talhoffer's and Paulus Kal's *fechtbucher*, excel at close-range thrusting, half-swording, armored combat, and quick follow up techniques like *Durchwechseln*.

Which of course begs the question, how did historical persons define and name their weapons? Where did they draw the lines? The short answer is that we do not really know because the historical terminology isn't very consistent across places, or over time, and manuals rarely feature dissimilar weapons used against each other.

I propose, however, that ancient warriors and teachers probably defined their weapons principally by the technique set possible with that weapon, and by the emphases of that technique set allowed by the design. Hypothetically, if you handed Ringeck an Oakeshott Type XIIIa and an Oakeshott XVIIIb and asked him what kind of weapons they were he would almost certainly answer, 'They are longswords.' He would also almost certainly add a few more descriptors, and some comments on the advantages of performing this or that technique with each one, but in the end, he'd probably claim that his fighting style would work with both. If you handed Fabris what is commonly known as a '*Pappenheimer*'-style rapier and a French three-ring rapier, and asked him what the weapons were, he'd say they were '*spada*' and that his style would work with both, though there might be this or that advantage of using one or the other. The point is that most of the details in a sword's design, if they do not change its fundamental form, will not actually make much difference to a dedicated martial artist in the way they will use the weapon. If on the other hand you handed Ringeck and Fabris each other's weapons they would say they were fundamentally different and that they couldn't use their art effectively with them.

Why should this be the case? The answer is simple. One can instantly know just by looking at and hefting a weapon if it can adequately perform the techniques used in a particular system. If it can, then it is that weapon. Many large swords of 50–54in (127–137cm) length are perfectly able to perform the techniques of every master I have read who stated they were teaching the 'longsword' of the Liechtenauer tradition. Once you move even a little beyond that, however, the weapons begin to lose the capability of performing many of the techniques which are central to longsword fighting, such as tightly controlled series of windings and thrusts at relatively close range, and swift reversals of direction to strike at different portions of the body in quick succession. Close-range half-swording becomes much more difficult, if not impossible, to perform with a sword that is 60in (152 cm) long.

For these reasons I argue that the possible technique set is what distinguishes the large two-handed swords of the *Landesknecht*, the Iberian *montante*, and other large two-hand swords, from large longswords. It is not so much the size, but the technique set available to the wielder that matters. Which is probably why ancient masters organized their manuals by weapon, rather than by technique, because the nature of the weapon defines the ultimate technique set that can be taught. In my experience size, or even the size of individual parts of longswords, can vary quite a bit until it changes the possibilities open to a user. The size of the user can also affect this a bit. Shorter people usually have difficulty using larger swords. Larger people may benefit from using larger swords, but plenty of large people I know make excellent use of shorter swords as well, so there is a fairly hard upper limit, but a rather vague lower limit. Phillipo Vadi recommended that a longsword should be able to be set straight up and down under the armpit, but that is just one master in one place and time. I suggest it is a good standard for a personal upper limit, but should not be thought of as an absolute hard and fast rule. Nor does it address the proportion, blade type, and other features of the sword for whatever style you intend to practice.[20]

The old classification systems give some idea of when and where the weapon was made. This helps us figure out which weapons were likely used by the masters we study, but that is as far as their benefits go. So, I will here offer my own system of classification, from the perspective of a swordsman. It is not wholly original, and these terms have been used by others previously, but, to my knowledge, this has never been properly codified. Because of inconsistency in historical naming conventions, the names I use here, though used in the period, will not correspond perfectly to all naming conventions in the era or across Europe. What I offer should be viewed as a modern naming system, based on historical terminology, to help an aspiring martial artist understand these weapons.

I propose that we should understand longswords as falling into three general categories. Their differences significantly influence the way you will fight, in spite of the technique set that they share. All these longsword types will work with Ringeck's art.

The first type is what I call the 'war sword.' Type XIIa, Type XIIIa and outliers of other types fall into this category. Mostly designed at the height of the age of mail, they excel at delivering powerful blows designed to defeat that kind of armor. They tend to be beefier than other longswords so that they can generate the power necessary to injure through mail. They also tend to move a little slower from technique to technique, but they are much more forgiving, and generally more powerful, when cutting. Though we find exceptions, war swords tend to be quite large relative to other longswords, and remained popular throughout the thirteenth and fourteenth century. The broad and shallow angled tips of these weapons make cuts with the tip comparably effective to cuts further down the blade in the same way the point of a saber or a katana tip does.

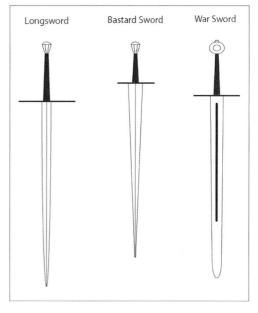

I call the second main type of longsword 'bastard swords.' Their makers optimized these weapons for armored combat. They are typically very short compared to other longswords, which makes them ideal for half-swording at close distances. They have very strong profile tapers which end in narrow points, ideal for thrusting into joints of armor. This also makes them very convenient for gripping the blade. The cross-section of the last few inches toward the point generally makes that portion of the blade unsuitable for cutting. You will often need to have at least four inches of the blade completely past the target in order to cut well. Bastard swords move very quickly, and many of them are light enough to use with one hand almost as well as a proper single-hand sword. Paulus Kal shows bastard swords being used in one hand with a buckler in the other, and Fiore dei Liberi shows them being used in one hand in some of his techniques, but this function is supplementary to its primary anti-armor features, and not necessarily true in all cases. Most models of the Oakeshott types XVa, XVIa, XVII and XVIIIa can be classified as bastard swords.

The third type is what I refer to as a 'longsword.' These weapons encompass the vast majority of other kinds of two-hand swords which were developed in Europe during the High Middle Ages and the Renaissance. These were optimized for civilian contexts where no armor was expected. Longswords served as sidearms, and particularly for unarmored fighting on foot, though against targets in mail or armor they would remain effective. They tend to have pointier profiles and be more point oriented in their fighting style than war swords. They move very quickly, are usually quite long, and have blades which are designed to cut through clothing very well. We often see significant curves in the edge in the weak of the sword where most cutting is done. They were particularly popular during the sixteenth and early seventeenth centuries. Both longswords and war swords are typically quite large, which makes them quite inconvenient to wield with a single hand. The very tips of longswords can be quite narrow, meaning that you will usually need at least two or three inches of blade past the point of contact to make effective cuts.

So what I call a 'longsword', in the sense of a general class of weapon that the sub-types fall into, is a double-edged weapon with a fairly long hilt ending with a pommel, with enough space on the handle for both hands to easily manipulate the weapon, a cross appropriately sized to protect the hands, usually about 9–13in (20–33cm), and a blade of typical length for the period, usually between 33–40in (80–100cm), which allows you to thrust along your opponent's blade or haft and stab them while remaining in contact with their weapon. I have seen specimens of longswords ranging through virtually all the possible combinations of those measurements. Though the shape of the hilt or pommel ranges widely and such variations do influence the way you can grip your sword a little, they do not matter much at all for determining the technique set. I strongly recommend finding a sword based on a historical weapon that you like, rather than a longsword design by a contemporary maker who did not directly examine historical weapons in making their design. I do not feel it is necessarily very valuable to mandate that everyone in a training group use the exact same kind of weapon, as long as the technique set their design makes possible is the same.

So, what type of longsword is most appropriate for students of Ringeck? Paulus Kal shows swords with blades and the pronounced points of the Oakeshott XVa variety, and he shows these weapons being used with one hand in his sword and buckler section. He again shows these same weapons in the armored combat sections of his work. This leads me to conclude that Kal, and probably his immediate predecessors and contemporaries, such as Ringeck, probably taught with bastard swords. The Goliath manual, on the other hand, comes from only a generation or so later, and shows very large weapons that are clearly a variety of war sword, or cutting oriented longsword. They are so big, in fact, that they border on the oversized two-handers made famous by the *Landesknecht*, which would not share the same technique set. While the bastard sword is most likely the weapon Ringeck had in mind when he taught the Duke of Bavaria and his men-at-arms, this is hardly absolute proof. Nor does it mean you must train with one. In point of fact, the Goliath manual is proof that variation was readily accepted within the tradition.

As a martial artist you must understand which kind of longsword you intend to learn how to use and the context it was optimized for. Make sure that you match your training equipment and whatever sword you buy to the type that you intend to master.

Chapter 8

Important Terms

I am going to define some simple terms so that you can understand the teachings that follow.

Absetzen

Literally translates to 'set aside'. It is used much less frequently than the word *Versetzen*, but, unfortunately, like the word *Versetzen*, it has no strong consistency in the way it is used. The powerful beating form of the *Krumphau* is called an *absetzen*, but so is the intercepting parry, which simultaneously thrusts, countering an opponent's thrust, in the section labeled *absetzen*.

Afterblow

A blow delivered moments after another strike or thrust has hit. Early modern and contemporary rules for tournaments usually penalize receiving one. They are designed to reflect situations where both parties would be injured, but sometimes, an afterblow that hits in sparring would be impossible in a real fight, and, unfortunately, which result would be the case cannot be known with any certainty.

Alber

Guard where the sword is extended forward and down so that the point rests near the ground. Its name translates to 'jester', 'fool', 'joker', or 'comedian'.

Cut, strike, blow, hew

These words refer to powerful strikes that are designed to cleave through portions of the body, leaving deep, life-threatening, wounds, or dismembering the target. Historically, the word strike, blow, or hew would be the rough equivalent of the word '*schlag*', and is also indicated by the suffix 'hau'.

Duplieren

Literally translated as 'doubling', or 'folding', this technique harasses an opponent by making a quick slice across the face, or a light blow to the head.

Durchlauffen
Literally translated as 'running through', this refers to the set of defensive grappling actions to throw or disarm an opponent taught near the end of the style.

Durchwechseln
Literally translated as 'changing through'. With longswords this is a risky move that disengages from your opponent's weapon, and makes a thrust to the other side.

Ochs
Guard where the sword is held just above the eyes extending toward the opponent's face. Its name translates to 'ox'.

Off-Hand
Usually the left hand. This hand goes on, or near, the pommel. It adds power and speed to the blow by snapping the blade forward, slicing action by helping pull the whole sword back along the plane of the cut, and provides a great deal of leverage. It is also instrumental in achieving good control.

Oberhau
A cut from above.

Mutieren
A *Winden* which thrusts to the lower quarters.

Nach
Literally 'after' it refers to needing to make a defense before one can attack.

Nachraisen
Though literally translated as 'travelling after', 'chasing' or 'pursuing' gives a better sense of the word's meaning. *Nachraisen* refers to an attack that takes advantage of a situation where your opponent has made a mistake, usually of gauging distance, giving you extra time to safely make an attack. Most of these opportunities happen during *Zufechten*.

Pflug
Guard where the sword is held near the rear hip on either side with the point aimed at the opponent's face. Its name means 'plough'.

Slice

This word refers to motions in which one presses the edge against the target, and pushes, or pulls, the edge across the target to cause a laceration. It also describes the effect of the point being raked across a target, usually the face. I use the term 'slice' as the direct equivalent of the German word '*schnitt*', and to describe the results of the technique *Duplieren*.

Stark

Literally 'strong', this is the portion of the blade that extends from the cross to the center of the blade. It is generally used for making defenses, as well as some slicing actions.

Sword hand/sword arm

This is the hand, and the arm of the respective hand, held close to the hilt. It is usually the stronger of your two hands. It directs the weapon, controls edge alignment, and does the principal motion of each action. For most people this is the right hand, and the book is written with that assumption. Just reverse the directions if you are left-handed.

Swach

Literally 'weak', this is the portion of the blade that extends from the center to the point. It is generally used for the primary cutting and thrusting actions.

Unterhau

A cut from below.

Vom Tag

Guard where the sword is held either on the shoulder, or above the head, with the point directed up and back. Its name literally translates 'from the roof' or 'from the day'.

Vor

Literally 'before', it refers to having the opportunity to attack with relative safety or control of the opponent.

Versetzen

Literally translated, it means 'setting aside'. It functions as a rough equivalent for the English word 'parry'. Ringeck used this word for several different types of defense, and it does not readily communicate whether the action is used to intercept, beat, or block an opponent's attack. We must look to context for this information.

Winden
Literally translated as 'winding', this is an action where the weapon is rotated and moved to achieve a position of greater leverage to parry an attack, and simultaneously make a thrust.

Zufechten
Literally translated as 'toward the fight'. This is the approach phase, where the opponents begin too far away to make any effective attacks, and close with each other so they can fight.

Chapter 9

Training Equipment

Historical clothing and training equipment differed somewhat from the modern. The clothing most often depicted in the manuals of the period is either their regular everyday clothing, or stripped-down versions of such clothing. Historical clothing incorporated designs that allowed for the full range of motion for the shoulders, legs, hips, groin, elbows and torso. When made properly, the shirts, doublets, and hose worn by people of the time proved much less restrictive than most modern clothes.

Quality swords and training swords are a must. I hate to think of all the training weapons I have been disappointed with, or broken, over the past two decades. Do not try to skimp on a real sword. In my experience people are much happier when they invest in a good quality training tool rather than getting a cheap one.

Preparing to train in the modern day requires clothing that gives us our full range of motion for our arms, legs, and torso. Most groups, including mine, do not require historical clothing, and it makes little difference for the execution of the technique.

I recommend the makers listed below not because they are the only good makers of training equipment out there, but because I have personal experience with their products, and found them excellent value for the money. Consult with your local group to decide on your training equipment.

Swords

Every serious practitioner of swordsmanship should own a sword and train with it as much as possible. The sword market today is much better than it used to be. There are many production and custom makers who make excellent and high quality swords. If your chief concern is historical accuracy though, it can be hard to find good documentation as to the accuracy of the designs used. Albion Swords, found at http://www.albion-swords.com makes high quality, readily available swords with well-documented research behind them. Their designs are based on some of the most detailed and best-documented hands-on research with historical swords in collections in Europe by Peter Johnsson. Tod's Workshop, found at: https://todsworkshop.com/ also makes thoroughly researched, highly accurate, weapons in close connection with Britain's finest collections.

Training swords

There are many good makers of training swords these days. Albion Swords makes excellent training swords. These can be found at http://www.albion-swords.com. I've also been very impressed by Szymon Chlebowski's training swords, which may be found at https://hemasupplies.com/ if you live in the US, or from his website: https://szymonchlebowski.pl/?v=d8e3950b4591 if you live almost anywhere else.

Wooden wasters

While historically accurate, at least in the medieval and Renaissance British milieu, wooden wasters are at best a stopgap for budget purposes. Having said this, I have used them extensively and some of my students begin their training with wooden wasters while they save up for better training equipment. Duncan Arms at https://www.duncanarms.com/ makes the best wooden wasters that I have personally handled. If you're going to go this route then I strongly recommend their 'hand and a half' wasters. The term 'hand and a half' is not a historically accurate term, but it is what they call them. Their 'Claymore' wasters are of dimensions which approximate the weapons shown in the Goliath manual, and it is perfectly possible to do all the techniques described in Ringeck's manual with wasters of that size , if you are large enough to handle one. These are strictly inferior to steel training swords, and the Liechtenauer tradition's iconography features steel training swords prominently.

Plastic wasters

After using these alongside wooden wasters and steel training swords for some years I have come to believe that there is only one place in which plastic wasters offer us a truly superior training experience: pell training. Plastic wasters, unlike wooden or steel training swords, will not permanently deform or break after very long use on a pell.

Competition gambeson/jacket

The vast majority of gambesons and jackets I have seen work pretty well. Any of the major brands will serve as long as they fit and give appropriate room for full shoulder motion.

Training jackets

I am quite partial to Jessica Finley's Ringen jackets because they can do double duty for grappling and swordplay. I use these as the standard uniform for my club.

Gloves

Leather gloves can make a surprising difference for comfort and mitigating the minor scrapes and bumps that happen during sword practices. Some manuals show their subjects wearing gloves, most do not. Whether or not you wear them is up to you. Many gloves come with a slippery coating that is designed to protect the leather and you will need to work with them for a while before they will work well in practice.

Pants/trousers

Any good pair of sufficiently flexible exercise pants will do just fine. Wear them high on your body so the seam goes well up into the crotch area. This will allow the pants to accommodate the large angles that happen in swordplay.

Historical clothing

I do not use historical clothing on a regular basis in my club. I have them for the purposes of experimentation, and for public presentations. If you are going for historically accurate clothing you are in for a fairly hefty investment of time and/ or money. Some makers who claim to offer 'historical clothing' or 'period garb,' do not actually offer accurate clothing. You are more likely to have your outfit fit into a fantasy movie than a *fechtbuch* unless you do serious research. You can get historical clothing off the rack, but even if the accuracy is good the fit can be tricky.

Your best bet for highly accurate historical clothing is to find a local tailor and get them to work from a pattern from a group or company that researches historical clothing and designs patterns based on them. I recommend www.patternsoftime. com as a good place to start. Experienced tailors I've worked with have told me that historical patterns are often somewhat hard to understand because the historical garments are so different from modern ones. It may take some practice and several tries to get things right. My own historical kit is not perfect, and has flaws that I intend to remedy.

Shoes

Any kind of shoe with a thin flat sole is fine. I have not, however, noticed a significant difference between modern shoes and historical shoes when I have used them, except in one major area: sole thickness. The thicker the sole of a shoe the more it distorts your footwork, and historical shoes all have very thin soles.

Sparring gloves

These pieces of protective gear are required at most modern tournaments. I do not feel that they should feature largely in our training because they are ahistorical and their size, and the limitations they place on the motion of our hands, often prevent you from learning how to use your strong and cross to defend your hands properly. They can, however, play an important role in learning intent and follow-through for strikes that specifically attack the hands and wrists. There are many great models. I can recommend the SPES Heavy Gloves and the Koenig Gloves from St Mark.

Chapter 10

Cutting with a Longsword

Learning to cut from a book is very difficult. Nothing less than practicing with a real sword in the air and on good targets will give you the skill to cut well. You need to own a good sword and use it regularly. Good teachers prove invaluable here because they can spot ways to improve your body mechanics early on, accelerate your learning, and prevent bad habits.

Grip the sword with your sword hand on the hilt and align the long edge with the knuckles of the first digit of your fingers. Maintain about 2–3cm between your hand and the crossguard. This will allow the sword to rock forward in your hand comfortably, allowing your index finger to extend a little when the sword moves forward. This space also helps the hilt protect your hand better. The thumb should press against the side of the grip, or, during specific techniques, be placed on the back or side of the grip in direct opposition to the fingers. This hand, and the wrist and arm behind it, guide the sword. The other hand should be placed lower on the grip or even on the pommel itself to add speed, impetus, and leverage. The grip of the off-hand will vary a great deal depending on what action you choose to take.[21]

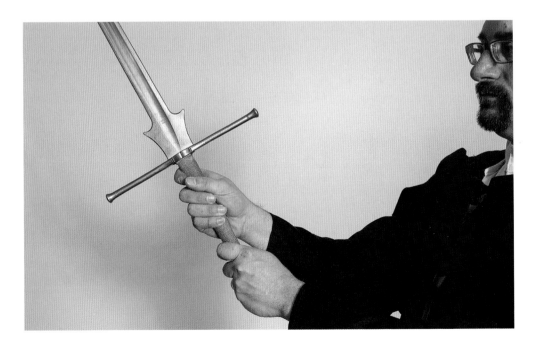

Ten major factors influence the effectiveness of a cut: the shape of the edge bevel, the curvature of the blade, the hardness of the edge, the fineness of the edge, the force of the strike, the straightness of the strike, the alignment of the edge, the slicing motion of the blade, the angle of the blade during the cut, and the motion of the body propelling the cut. Four of these factors are determined by the design, sharpness, and quality of your sword. The other six factors come from the wielder, and in my experience a good swordsman can usually cut very well with a mediocre sword as long as it is sharp.

Cross-section

There are four main types of cross-sections that longswords use: diamond, lenticular, hollow ground, and hexagonal. The blade's cross section determines the shape and angles of the surfaces where the planes of the blade meet at the edge. The wider the angle of the edge, the more forgiving the blade will be while cutting, and the narrower the angle, the more cutting potential the weapon will be able to achieve.

Diamond cross-sections define most bastard swords. Their design achieves maximum stiffness, and very narrow points perfect for thrusting at the small gaps in armor. As the cross-section narrows towards the point the cutting capability is

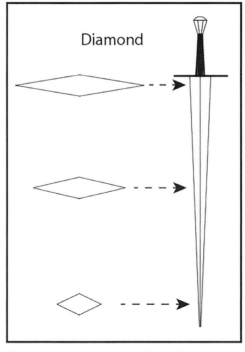

Diamond cross-section bastard sword.

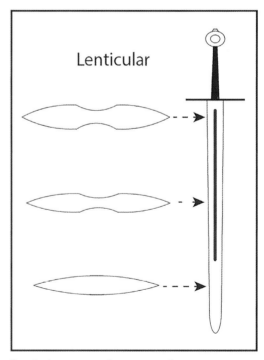

Lenticular cross-section war sword.

sacrificed to achieve the specialized anti-armor point. The middle and base of the blade become very wide and can have tremendous cutting potential because of the acute angles, but they are often quite sensitive to bad cutting technique. They have the quickest and most accurate points of any sword design used by man and rely more on quick and sophisticated point work than other longswords in a civilian setting, but they can still remove heads or limbs with relative ease.

Designed in the age of mail, lenticular cross-sections dominated the early longsword designs of the 1200s and 1300s. They create comparatively wide angles at the edges but the curved planes offer lower friction along the often very wide blades behind them. This design results in powerful, aerodynamic shapes that are very forgiving of mediocre cutting technique and robust enough to stand up to repeated use on hard targets. Their comparatively heavy blades make for amazing cutting swords and produce very consistent results. Their broad points cut almost as well as the rest of the blade, allowing them to strike farther out than other swords. Their comparatively large fullers add strength by slightly thickening the blade and increasing its stiffness, especially in the *stark* (strong, the portion nearest the cross) which does the bulk of the defensive work. This also helps make sure that the sword cuts the target rather than flexing.

The term hollow ground is a misnomer from modern methods of making such weapons. What we really have are blades with diamond cross-sections that have very wide fullers pounded into their flat surfaces in order to use the material as efficiently as possible. This allows these weapons to be longer on average than other longswords. While these weapons often have moderately wide edges and comparatively thick ridges the lack of surface area in contact with the target offsets these factors in cutting. Their length, relative lightness for their size, their excellent cutting capabilities, and nimble points make them arguably the best design for civilian settings, but we also see many of them in conjunction with warfare and military men. Many longswords with these cross sections also include narrow diamond-shape tips that serve excellently for fighting armored targets. Many of these swords also feature prominent curves in the

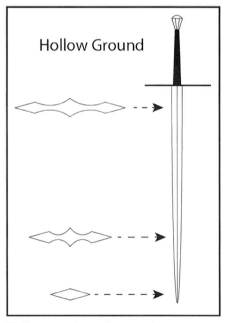

Hollow ground cross longsword.

blade near the prime cutting portion of the blade, further improving their cutting capability. Little if any distal taper happens on the edge bevels which makes them more forgiving to mediocre cutting technique.

Hexagonal cross-sections come in two varieties: bastard sword and longsword. The bastard sword designs often cut very poorly toward the point, but their lower friction from perfectly perpendicular surfaces to the angle of the cut can make them excellent cutters closer to the hilt. The longsword designs have very little friction and their comparatively wide blades often cut very well. Like the diamond cross-section bastard sword, hexagonal bastard swords' cross-sections become more equilateral toward the point, but the longsword versions taper only slightly, and the prime cutting portion near the tip also tends to thin slightly to increase its cutting potential.

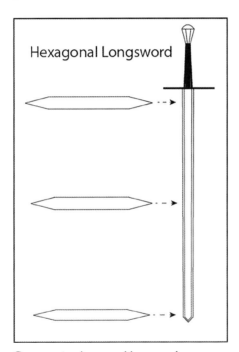

Cross-section hexagonal longsword.

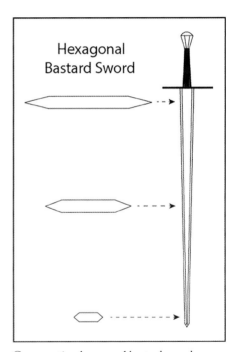

Cross-section hexagonal bastard sword.

Curvature of the blade

A curved blade has slightly less material to cut through in order to reach the mid-point of a target. This superior efficiency holds true until the weapon gets to the center of the target. The more curved the weapon is, the better it cuts until the curvature of the blade exceeds the curvature of its target, which never happens with traditional sword designs. After reaching the center of the target curved swords become less efficient on the way out, and, if they finish cutting the target, they will have used the exact same amount of energy as a straight blade. Depth of penetration up to the center of the target is what matters most in a cut, because this allows you to get to the organs in the center of the body. Because of this, the greater the curvature of the blade, the easier the cut will be. The results are noticeable, but not dramatic: a sword curvature that actually mirrors your target only gets about 20% more efficiency until they hit the center of the target. Even very curved swords such as the shamshir or the kilij do not approach the curvature of cross-sections of human bodies. Most curved swords only gain 5–10% percent extra efficiency in the first half of their cutting actions. This does,

however, mean that curved swords are more likely to do significant damage if the cut doesn't have perfect execution. In spite of having straight blades many European swords in fact have curved edges or curved portions of their edges, which demonstrates understanding of this principle. Type XIVa and XVIIIa longswords often have this feature. Perhaps more important, curvature also enhances the slicing action which needs to occur in order to cut well by effectively angling the sword backward.

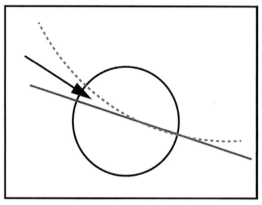

This diagram demonstrates the space saved by a particularly curved blade. Most curved sword blades have much less curvature.

Fineness of the edge

Under a microscope the edge of a sword will look like the edge of a saw. As a sword is pushed or pulled through the target thousands of tiny teeth on the edge will saw through the target. The finer the teeth, the less work that needs to be done by each tooth, and the better the cut. The fineness of the edge that can be achieved is determined by the composition of the edge. It is also determined in great measure by the skill of the sharpener. I do not know of any substantial statistical work on the fineness of historical sword edges, or other work establishing what level of grit works best for particular contexts, but I hope someday someone does that research.[22]

Beneath a microscope a blade will show teeth like a saw: the smaller the teeth, the stronger their structure and the less material each tooth has to cut.

Hardness of the edge

Harder materials can be given finer edges, making them more efficient when cutting and slicing. If, however, you get an edge that is too hard the weapon will be brittle, and prone to chip, crack, or even break. Balancing the need for a hard, fine edge and a strong blade has been a conundrum of sword design that has been solved in a number of ways over the centuries and across the world.

The slicing motion of the blade

A sword's blade moves on an arcing path when cutting and will naturally be pushed or pulled through the target. You can greatly increase this effect with your slicing technique. This will help sever the fibrous structures of sinew and clothing. With

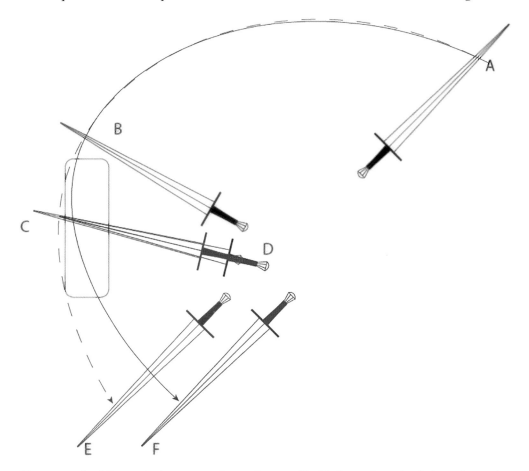

Here we see the difference in the motion of a sword in a cut. The black sword at point A shows the starting position. The black sword at point B represents the weapon's position at the point of maximum extension just before contact. The red line and swords show the course of the weapon as it travels without pulling the blade to improve the slicing action through points C and E. The blue line and swords trace the course of the sword as it moves with superior slicing action through points D and F.

practice one can dramatically increase the amount of push or pull by subtly changing the vectors, angles, and curvature of the cut by adjusting the extension of the joints of the arms, wrists, and hands before and after contact is made.

Alignment of the edge

If the edge is aligned incorrectly with the plane of the cut, some or most of the force of the strike will be absorbed by the weapon, which is manifested in flexing, bouncing, or potentially in damage to the blade, such as chipping, cracking, bending or breaking, or it will be transmitted to the target as blunt force, and the cut will not penetrate deeply.

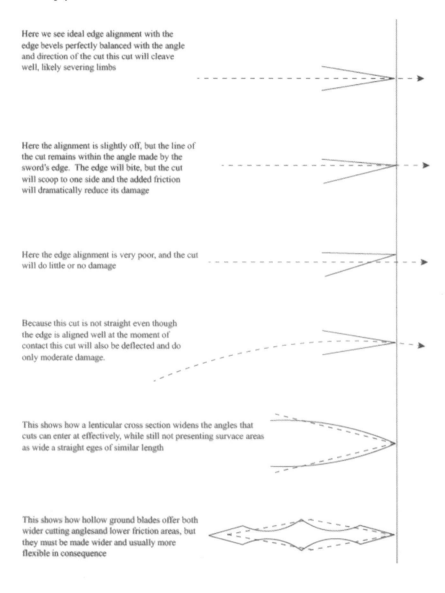

Here we see ideal edge alignment with the edge bevels perfectly balanced with the angle and direction of the cut this cut will cleave well, likely severing limbs

Here the alignment is slightly off, but the line of the cut remains within the angle made by the sword's edge. The edge will bite, but the cut will scoop to one side and the added friction will dramatically reduce its damage

Here the edge alignment is very poor, and the cut will do little or no damage

Because this cut is not straight even though the edge is aligned well at the moment of contact this cut will also be deflected and do only moderate damage.

This shows how a lenticular cross section widens the angles that cuts can enter at effectively, while still not presenting survace areas as wide a straight eges of similar length

This shows how hollow ground blades offer both wider cutting anglesand lower friction areas, but they must be made wider and usually more flexible in consequence

Straightness of the strike

The motion of a cut forms an arcing plane. If this plane is not straight it will not cut well because it will waste the energy of the strike once it connects by pushing against the material with portions of the blade that do not cut and in directions that will not cause the object to be divided by the sword's edge.

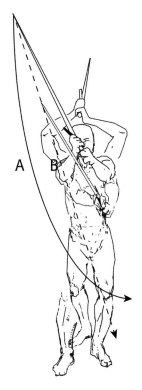

Here Line A represents the plane of the sword's cut being lined up perfectly once the sword has reached the desired angle. If the cut is executed this way then the blade will cut well, and cleanly, usually bisecting any reasonable target if the edge is aligned with the plane. Line B on the other hand shows that plane scooping underneath the desired line. When this happens, the sword will turn in the target losing most of its inertia and cease to cut. Usually cuts made this way will leave superficial damage, even if the edge is very sharp.

Angle of the blade during the strike

The steeper the angle of the blade vis-a-vis your target the less work must be done by each portion of the blade as it cuts through the target. The greater the angle the more efficient the cut will be. A steep angle also improves the slicing motion of the blade. Maintaining too steep an

Because of the roughly circular motions of swords, holding a sword at a steeper angle will accentuate the slicing action of the blade as it moves through the target. The red sword demonstrates a blade at the point of maximum extension. This will minimize the slicing factors and prevent the weapon from cutting to its maximum effect. This angle does have the maximum reach, but it comes at a high cost of cutting capability. The black sword demonstrates a more common angle at point of contact, this will allow some slicing factors to occur with only slightly reduced reach. The blue sword shows making contact at a very steep angle, the slicing factor will be highly enhanced if this is your point of maximum extension, though this can only be achieved with a significant reduction of reach.

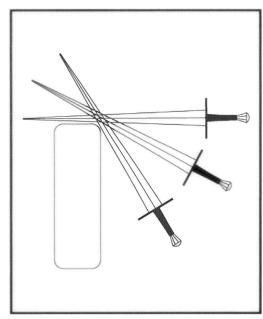

angle, however, will greatly diminish your reach, make it more difficult to accelerate the strike to good cutting speeds, diminish the amount of rotation achieved before reaching the target, and reduce its force at the point of impact by generating a transverse force with some of the energy, but this last factor only applies against hard targets. This can be enhanced to a certain extent by having a blade with steeply angled edges, such as Oakeshott type XVa swords, which seem to have been popular in Ringeck's time. Curved edges also naturally increase the angle of the blade during the strike.

The motion of the body propelling the strike

Liechtenauer said 'Always fight with all your strength', which we usually take to mean never go easy on an opponent, but another way to understand this is by analysis of the body mechanics of the actions you make, so that your whole body contributes to its effect. While cutting the sword is connected to your body, and your entire body can, and should, move in a way that helps the cut. The extension of the legs, turning the hips and shoulders, extending the arms at the elbows and wrists, and the motion of the step, should all be used to propel the weapon along its desired path. Take a good look at the examples below.

Paulus Kal's cutting technique keeps the sword close to the body and the posture very upright with small footwork and straight legs. This lets the torso and arms press powerfully down and forward at close distances.

Talhoffer's structure tends to use a very wide stance with arms that are strongly extended out and on a slight downward angle to maximize reach.

The Goliath manual shows larger footwork, extended arms, with upright body posture, and moderate leaning of the torso. We often see stepping across the line. By turning the forward foot toward the opponent and bending the knees the body's weight supports the downward motion of the sword.

The Glasgow version of Ringeck's manual shows footwork that uses strong lateral angles with a low center of gravity allowing the weight of the body to push the weapon in the desired direction while the blade extends forward, similar to, but not as extreme, as what we see in Talhoffer's manual, and with more lateral motion.

Force of the strike

The blade of a sword is a wedge-shaped object being driven through material when cutting; the harder it strikes the deeper the cut. This is particularly important when developing the force to cut bones. It is also important when striking a well-protected opponent, such as one wearing a gambeson or mail. A forceful strike to the head of an armored opponent may be unlikely to kill, but it may very well disorient them. Adding extra snap with the off-hand on the pommel is the best way to improve this with a longsword. Note that if the weapon is rotated too far it can compromise the slicing motion of the blade and decrease the weapon's efficiency at cutting sinew and clothing. It can also compromise the structure of the wrists.[23]

I would like to make one final point about generating force. European swords from the Middle Ages and Renaissance use pommels in their design to affect the force of their cuts, not just their center of gravity. Pommels greatly increase the force of a cut, by as much as twenty percent. This only occurs if the blade is snapped forward to add rotation in the hand. Hanko Dobringer describes this in his manual on page 15r of his manuscript. This fact, coupled with the starting and ending positions he shows, requires some snapping rotation at the wrist. Joachim Meyer teaches that the sword should move through a position which he calls 'Long Point', and his depiction of this position shows the sword very extended, and the wrists quite bent. So ancient masters knew that snapping the sword forward could make a cut more effective when done properly, and they used a sword design that was optimized for that kind of motion.

While most earlier masters do not depict quite as much extension as later masters like Meyer, they nevertheless cut much farther out from the body than you find in other forms of swordsmanship where they do not use swords with large pommels. Manuals from the Liechtenauer tradition, with the notable exception of Paulus Kal, clearly depict relatively extended snapping motions bringing the pommel up near the right forearm during the cut and ending in a relatively extended position with the point near the ground. Good slicing action needs to be paired with this snapping action, but, if used with good edge control offers superior reach, and force.

Kal's technique works on the opposite principles, using almost no snap of the wrist in order to maintain a steep angle throughout the cut and emphasize the slicing action. So, precedent for both types of striking technique exists within Liechtenauer's tradition. Whether you use one method, the other, or both, the most important thing is to make your practice consistent, and do your best with the style you choose.

Getting all these factors to line up well is the essence of skilled cutting. Different kinds of swords use different principles to different extents, as do different fighting styles. Not all swords are designed to cut exactly the same way. It takes a great deal of practice to learn to cut well with the swords you choose to practice with, and you should do it every day.

Chapter 11

Learning New Techniques

I use four phases for teaching techniques, concepts, and strategies. I begin with what I call ideal forms. In these drills the participants execute each action after the initial engagement to their natural stage of completion according to a pre-arranged drill before the response happens. This allows them to see what each movement would accomplish, and it allows them to practice it without the pressure of immediate response. As a student advances it becomes important to return to and practice ideal forms to perfect the technique, as well as to remind them of the goal of each action. This type of training can also be done much faster, and with a much higher level of safety, because there are no surprises. Because each action is done and completed before the response is given the students can use the predictability of the drill to push their levels of control, which is the best way to improve a student's control. This kind of drilling remains very valuable for advanced students as well as for new students.

Second, I teach my students to do the drill with feeling. The drill remains choreographed, but with a major change. I instruct the students to do each technique with as much intent and commitment as they safely can. They must do it as fast as they can while remaining in control. At each bind the student whose turn it is to respond must respond realistically to what they feel, and, to a lesser extent, what they see, with the prescribed response. In this phase they should be learning to notice the signals that indicate they should do a new action. Many of these drills flow naturally into branches where a student needs to make a choice about which move to do next, and this form of practice helps them make those decisions more quickly and accurately. Most importantly, if they do not feel the correct situation happen, for whatever reason, the drill should be reset, rather than trying to make adjustments after the fact to force a situation to work.

Third, I introduce a limited form of sparring. The initial techniques are still prescribed, but the students are allowed to follow what they feel, and to vary from the drill beyond each of their first moves. Ideally, they will use the techniques I have been teaching them at the correct moments and for the correct contexts as they encounter them.

Fourth, once a student is prepared for sparring, I introduce sparring matches as a way of pressure testing their learning. At unplanned times, I, and the more experienced students, will deliberately attempt to give them the situations we have been training them for. If they succeed at feeling and responding correctly then they have achieved at least a basic level of mastery of the technique.

PART II

Ringeck's *Fechtbuch*

Lesson 1: Ringeck's Introduction

Translation

Here begins the teaching of the recital
Herein is written knightly the art of the longsword, created and organized by Johannes
Liechtenauer, a great master of the art. By God's mercy he had this recital of his art written
in obscure and secret words to prevent it becoming commonly known. The aforementioned
words are herein interpreted and taught by Sigmund Ringeck, who is also a great master
of this art, who served as Schiermeister to the highborn Prince Albrecht Pfalzgraf of the
Rhine, Herzog, and Bavaria. He interpreted these secret words in this book, so that a
trained fighter may examine it, and understand this art.

Here begins the recital
Young knight, learn
to love god, and honor women
Thus, your honor will grow.
Practice chivalry, learn
the arts that ennoble you
and bring you honor in war.
Wrestle well with good holds,
learn the lance, spear, sword, and messer manfully,
and spoil them in other's hands.
Strike true, and hard there.
Rush to meet your foe,
and whether you hit or not, fight on,
and the wise will envy you.
Always remember this,
All arts have length and measure. (Rostock manuscript)

Theory: honor, god, and women

The first teachings of Liechtenauer address why one would learn a martial art. He also indirectly implies when one would use it. In the medieval and Renaissance philosophies violence should only be used to defend that which was sacred, including king, country, home, family, and religion, and even then, theoretically, only in what they called an honorable fashion, respecting the laws and customs of their time. While such ideas were by no means followed by everyone, or anywhere near as broadly as the writers of the time might have preferred, the fact that Liechtenauer pays homage to these values plays an important role in learning this art.

Liechtenauer's list is by no means exhaustive, nor is his poetry a treatise on the appropriate place of violence in society, but the general points he raises echo throughout other manuals and writings of his time. If we take them at their word, then they attempted to instill in their students, who are assumed to be male, a philosophy which would motivate them to defend their religion, women, and to live by the ideals of chivalry. Chivalry was a fairly amorphous term, and seems to have been the result of popular literature just as much as religious tenets or formal codes of knightly orders. Nevertheless, they took the ideal seriously and used it as one of the foundations for their concepts of right behavior. Chivalry theoretically promoted courage, loyalty to king, country and family, honesty, courteousness, being true to one's word, and generosity.

Chivalric ideals sought to breed restraint and a sense of duty as protectors in young warriors. A warrior could have thousands of hours of training in martial arts by the time they reached their twenties, and often could not be easily restrained by peacekeepers in the Middle Ages and Renaissance. The fact that members of the fighting classes often held positions in government, and acted as enforcers and adjudicators of law, exacerbated this difficulty. The advocates of chivalry and religion argued that these values helped curb the wanton violence that such young men were capable of.[24]

Liechtenauer and his successors aimed to inspire the students they led to use his teachings in the defense of these sacred things. First, they admonished their 'young knight' to love God, implying that the group should value and be willing to defend their religion. His admonition to revere women might seem misogynistic to modern sensibilities, but it reflects the exclusivity of these teachings, and implicitly acknowledges a reality in which the vast majority of women are physically weaker than men, and therefore often needed protection. It was true then, and is true today, that women are often the victims of violent crime because they are generally physically weaker than their attackers, and predators feel emboldened by that fact.

It is easy to look at the statement about women and see it only from our modern perspective. We should be willing to try to take these men at their word on the subject of women. The mandate to revere women meant a great deal to them and their relationship to women formed a core part of their identity. In their time family life developed inextricably with public and political life. Family life centered on women, and the children who were born to their families. What Renaissance people would have seen as women's work: organizing their homes, taking care of household finances, bearing and raising their children, and cooking meals, all of which was far more time-consuming that it is now, made the world go round, so to speak. This admonition stands as just one among many from authors of that time period to respect, honor, and defend women. Women represented the foundation of family, clan, and therefore honor and joy in life, and, in spite of popular perceptions about the looseness of morals in the Middle Ages and Renaissance, people were consistently taught to consider the marriage relationship sacred, and many did. A great percentage, perhaps a majority, of the duels fought from the Middle Ages to the nineteenth century, including the last duel authorized by the French parliament, were fought over women's honor.[25]

In the medieval and early Renaissance periods women exercised somewhat more freedom than they did in the late Renaissance and Early Modern periods, and there is some evidence, albeit often limited in scope, or anecdotal, that they participated in some martial activities on rare occasions. The objections in Renaissance books on courtesy to women being taught martial arts imply that women may sometimes have been taught these arts, hence the need to prohibit the practice. The figure of Walpurgis in the earliest fight-book known, the *I.33*, seems to have been a woman, and this implies that a very few women may have learned some of the fighting arts of the time, at least for self-defense. Talhoffer's fight-book depicts teaching women fighting techniques for specialized duels. So, in spite of the overt male orientation of the martial societies, and the attempts to exclude women from them, it may not have always been so clear cut in practice.

Next Liechtenauer comes to the subject of honor. Honor meant mutual respect from one's peers, as well as personal satisfaction with one's own conduct. Its public and private dimensions could be quite complex. Essentially though, by fulfilling one's role in society, by succeeding in one's endeavors, by keeping one's word, protecting one's place, family, king, and country, and by conducting oneself according to the traditions and customs deemed worthy of respect, one obtained both forms of honor. By contrast, failure without worthy effort, neglecting one's duties, breaking one's word, allowing a slight (which is different from simple embarrassment), would bring dishonor. Conduct unbecoming one's station brought dishonor. Extreme situations of public or private dishonor could lead to legal action, dueling, feuds, or even private warfare.

Warfare, the next subject Liechtenauer speaks of, had evolved quite a bit since the early medieval era. By this time the feudal system no longer formed the primary basis of militaries as monarchs consolidated their hold on their countries and provinces, and city-states simultaneously asserted their own independence. Remember, the Renaissance is as far removed in time from the early feudal era of the early Middle Ages as it is from modern armies which use fighter jets and mechanized tanks. Nevertheless, a warrior's performance in combat, and the rewards of social station and wealth they could win, were directly related to their training in the martial arts.

Success on the battlefield, and even honorable performance in the face of defeat, brought them respect from their civic leaders, overlords, and the patrons who paid their bills.

From time to time I find someone citing the tradition of capturing opponents for ransom as a point against the deadliness of European martial arts. I would like to respond that European history is quite clear that in spite of the traditions of capturing enemies for ransom, the exigencies of combat often resulted in death and maiming. Certainly, the Liechtenauer tradition, and insofar as I have been able to discover, all other European martial arts which state that they are intended for dueling and warfare, are full of techniques designed to cause immediate maiming or death. Capturing an armed and skilled opponent with years of training is no small task, and often could not be done alone, or during a chaotic battle. Liechtenauer's statement that practice of this art would bring honor in warfare implies that skill at arms allowed a fighter to defeat his enemies, achieve tactical and strategic objectives, acquit himself well, and stand as an equal among his peers. Capturing an opponent is not specifically mentioned anywhere in the corpus of his tradition. In addition, many of these arts were designed for the dueling field where death was the very goal of the event, and there is a strong argument to be made that Liechtenauer's longsword art, in spite of the mention of warfare in the initial language, was optimized for dueling.

Despite the overt statements about chivalry, and the language aiming Liechtenauer's teachings at the nobility, and the fact that many of Liechtenauer's successors, including Ringeck, did teach some very famous noblemen, many of the inheritors of his tradition do not seem to have come from the upper classes, or to have taught them exclusively. The later masters especially seem to have come from middling classes, and to have taught those classes of professionals as well. They more often served as fight masters to guilds than knightly patrons, and they disseminated these teachings quite widely. Some of these prominent practitioners and teachers are known to have learned trades, or served in public office, and taught and practiced martial arts on the side.[26]

Theory: the underlying strategy

For the purposes of learning the techniques and fighting style I wish to stress these introductory lines:

> *'Strike true and hard there. Rush to meet your foe, and whether you hit or not, fight on, and the wise will envy you.'*

All the writers of Liechtenauer's tradition emphasize taking and maintaining the offensive against an opponent. Dobringer argued strenuously, and at length, that in his experience simply seizing the initiative and attacking first often won fights in spite of an opponent's superior skill or training. Ringeck echoes this teaching in his writing more briefly. Nearly every Liechtenauer defense is designed to instantly cut or thrust in the same motion as a defense. Every action bears the goal of attacking or gaining an opportunity to attack.[1]

Liechtenauer and Ringeck did not, however, teach a reckless form of swordsmanship. In their fighting style you constantly seek the enemy's openings, but never in a way that exposes you. Everything should be done at the correct time, at the correct distance, and with a technique that secures your safety. With only a few exceptions, you should be seeking your opponent's openings rather than waiting for them to come at you.

Perhaps even more importantly the words '*whether you hit or not, fight on, and the wise will envy you*' teach us a great deal about the strategy they employed. The forms and drills they taught move rapidly, seamlessly and continuously, from one offense to another. If and when an opponent successfully defends an attack, the student of this tradition will simply apply the techniques they have learned with the principles of 'Before' (*Vor*), 'After' (*Nach*), 'In the Moment' (*Indes*), 'Weak' (*Schwech*) and 'Strong' (*Stark*), all of which will be explained later, and continue their offense. With these principles we will always bring to bear another threat in a manner that continues to secure our own safety, either by forcing our opponent to respond to our threat before they can make their own attack, or by creating additional space and time in which to attack them cleanly. Ideally, the Liechtenauer fighter flows from attack to attack and never gives their opponent the breathing room they need until they fail to make a defense, and are defeated.

This first lesson advocates a highly aggressive strategy, which continues the aggression of the first attack with subsequent attacks. Ringeck and Liechtenauer placed these here at the front for one simple reason: victory, ultimately, comes from attacking. Keeping yourself safe with secure technique and control of distance is absolutely necessary to a successful fighting style, but you cannot win unless, and until, you attack. Dobringer says that the opposite approach – waiting for your opponent to attack so that you can strike in the opening created during or after the attack – is quite dangerous against a skilled fighter, because you must first deal with the lethal threat they present, and if they pursue you long enough, or if they

---

1. Dobringer, Hanko, Pol Hausbuch, MS 3227a, Germanes Nationalmuseum, Nuremburg, pgs. 16r–16v, 20r–22v.

get close enough, the speed of your reactions may not be sufficient. They may be able keep you on the defensive, and prevent you from getting through with your own techniques. Playing defense also requires much greater capacity to read the opponent, choose the appropriate counter-technique, and execute it quickly enough for it to have its desired effect. It is not a strategy that generally works well for the beginner.[2]

Logically, therefore, you should always seek to be striking your opponent, especially when you must use a defense. In this style the threat you need to present must be embedded in the defense, or the opponent can ignore it and attack again.

Theory: all arts have length and measure

Unfortunately, neither Ringeck, nor later masters of his tradition, expound in depth on the principles of length and measure, and it is impossible to fight well without them. Attacking when your opponent is out of reach can be suicidal. Choosing an attack for a distant opponent when they are too close will not work well either. We must seek beyond Ringeck's text for answers and constantly strive to improve our understanding of length and measure throughout our training in creative ways. In my club we always begin well out of distance, and use an approach phase in every drill, sparring match, or other activity, to ensure that we learn length and measure in what the Liechtenauer tradition calls *Zufechten*, or the approach to the fight.

A good practitioner of this art must know exactly what kind of strike is able to harm an opponent, with the weapons they are using, at the distance they are at. They must gauge how much they can extend while avoiding overextension. The arms must remain slightly bent at the elbows during the strike, and the hands should bend forward a little and let the sword move forward in the grip, but they should not move past the point where you can keep a secure grip, and maintain a powerful structure. The body must be able to extend and support the strike with its motion and weight. The cut must have enough blade making contact to cleave well, and thrusts must penetrate to a sufficient depth. Once you know this you can choose your position, path of approach, and mode of attack. The other side of this principle is knowing when your opponent can threaten you, and what techniques they can threaten you with from the position they are in. Combining these two sets of knowledge yields a truly formidable fighter who can control the fight by controlling the distance, and the way the distance changes as the fight unfolds. Learning length and measure requires understanding the length and speed of our stride, the way we extend our hands, and the size and design of our sword, as well as judging all of that for our opponent as well.

---

2. Ibid.

Our students must develop an intuitive grasp of length and measure, but in the beginning let them approach and measure distance by carefully extending their weapon as if they were striking. Examine the distance between their feet as well as their bodies and swords. Here Ben is demonstrating a distance beyond the extreme edge of what Silver called 'the place'. At this distance he cannot strike Randy without taking a step forward. If he were to attack here it would be easier for Randy to read the attack and make a defense because it takes longer to execute. I interpret this as too far for an effective attack.

Note the position of the body supporting the strike: slightly bent elbows, stance squared with the angle of engagement, and extension without over-extension in the hands.

I choose to derive my understanding of this instruction from Ringeck's later, terse, but very revealing, instructions: 'Close with your foe when you cut so you can work your will, and prevent *Durchwechseln* from penetrating your shield,' and 'When you come at him aim for his head and body. Close with him so that he cannot change through with his point in front of you' (see Lesson 3). From these statements we learn two things: that Ringeck wanted us to close to a particular distance with opponents in order to cut, and that cutting to the head and body at this distance would prevent our opponents from using *Durchwechseln*, a particularly quick and deadly technique, against us.

Durchwechseln, also known as a Disengagement in later English sword schools, and the *Cavazione* in Italian schools, features prominently in Ringeck's fighting theory. Ringeck clearly taught his students to never leave themselves open to this technique. He rightly feared, and taught his students to exploit, its speed and deadliness. He spends a relatively large amount of space, for him, in several parts of the manual, explaining how it works, and how to avoid leaving yourself open to it. Analysis of Ringeck's text makes two things are very clear. First, because longswords operate without a companion weapon *Durchwechseln* can only be safely attempted if the opponent is not immediately threatening you. Second, it also cannot be done if the distance is too close. Thrusts must strike vital organs to guarantee immediate effect, therefore *Durchwechseln* to the lower quarters must be reserved for particularly bad defenses; this means that one must attempt to focus these at the head and chest. If you are too close to conveniently move the blade around the opponent's weapons and body to thrust at the head and torso then you rob *Durchwechseln* of its chief advantage - its speed - and you may even make it impossible. This forces your opponent to use other techniques. This knowledge requires that we learn to fight at a very specific distance, and in a very specific way in Ringeck's system.

I derive some of my interpretation of the distance Ringeck intended us to engage at from George Silver's books. In good distance you can reach your opponent without stepping. Because I do not teach Silver, I do not use Silver's terminology, I usually call it 'close distance,' to echo Ringeck's language, or 'good distance,' as a qualitative name. One should not enter close distance, or permit the opponent to enter it, unless one immediately attacks in a secure and skilled manner. Most systems of sword-fighting approach this distance very differently than Ringeck, possibly including other teachers of the Liechtenauer tradition. I advocate this interpretation because the clues Ringeck gives do not leave room for variation on the subject, and I find myself persuaded of his logic. When we combine the strategy of continuous, but secure aggression, with this very close, but very effective, distance, we get a devastating form of offense. I will elaborate on this later as we get into the techniques.

Lesson 2: The General Lessons

This is the text of the general lessons of the longsword.

If you want to show you are skilled,
Then approach with the left foot, and cut with the right.
From left to right
Is the strongest way to fight.

This is the first lesson of the long sword: if you want to fight strongly and correctly then learn to strike all blows from both sides. If you want to cut from your right side, begin the cut with your left foot forward, and if you want to strike from the left side begin with the right foot forward. If you strike an Oberhau from the right side follow the blow with your right foot or the blow will be false and ineffective, because your right side drags behind. If you do not strike properly then the cut will fall short, because it cannot travel on its proper arc to end in front of the left foot.

Likewise, if you strike from the left, and you do not follow the blow with the left foot, it will also be wrong. So mark which side you will strike from, so that the foot will follow the cut, and lend it strength, and thus you will succeed in all techniques, and this is how you shall always cut. (The Dresden Manuscript)

Theory: historical footwork

The manuals from the Liechtenauer tradition and other contemporary traditions show quite a variety of steps and extension in their footwork. Talhoffer, for example, who seems to have had some cross-pollination with Liechtenauer's style in the mid-1400s, shows the most extreme footwork I have ever encountered, even in his armored combat sections. Some of the steps depicted in his manuals actually appear longer than the lunges of many rapier masters of the seventeenth century with the heel of the foot far ahead of the knee. Paulus Kal, on the other hand, despite being a contemporary of Talhoffer, and from the same general region, consistently depicts footwork akin to that which you would see in some surviving Japanese sword styles, using very small steps and a very upright posture. Between these two extremes we find all other fight books, some with larger, more dynamic footwork, some with smaller, more conservative footwork.

The other manuals of the Liechtenauer tradition: Hans Medel, Dobringer, the Goliath manual, Joachim Meyer, Paulus Hector Mair, and the Glasgow version of Ringeck, use quite a variety of extensions as well as varied weighting in their

This image shows a stance typical of the largest footwork in Talhoffer's manuals. The forward foot has the heel placed beyond the knee and the body is bent forward.

This image shows a stance typical of the footwork in Paulus Kal's manual.

footwork. We can, therefore, surmise that there was no uniformity in the size of the footwork taught by historical masters of this tradition, and while historical stepping was often relatively large, using much smaller steps, or even using them exclusively, was an effective contemporary style.

In the Liechtenauer tradition they typically used a centered or slightly forward weighted stance, especially when attacking, though Dobringer, Ringeck and Meyer also show rear-weighted stances, particularly with the *Ochs* guard, as well as in certain grappling situations. The iconography and texts do not always make absolutely clear as to whether, how far, or in which direction they stepped offline to attack. Attacking offline rather than straight on can allow one to attack from safer angles rather than direct or linear footwork, but it requires a closer distance be reached before launching the attack. When they step offline, they typically step to the side of the moving foot, though the

This image shows a stance with outturned feet.

This stance replicates Ringeck's footwork as it is typically shown in the Glasgow manual wide stances, but not as wide as Talhoffer's, and maintains an upright posture like Paulus Kal, though some forward bending of the torso is sometimes shown.

This image depicts a side oriented back weighted stance which appears in the Glasgow manual. This results most often from stepping laterally with the forward foot to that side.

depictions of many techniques show stepping across the center line to the side of the original forward foot instead. Some manuals depict stances with the feet turned away from each other, with bent knees and low centers of gravity somewhat similar to some of the 'horse' stances in some Asian martial arts, but many manuals do not show any such stances.

I have attempted to replicate these various kinds of footwork, using them exclusively for several months, and then mixing them up. This led me to the conclusion that any single restricted kind of footwork is completely viable against virtually any other footwork style. You just have to adjust your use of length and measure accordingly. Using two or more together also seems to work just fine, and is supported by treatises that depict such things, like Ringeck, Mair, and Talhoffer. I suggest experimenting, finding out your limits, and working on different surfaces, including natural surfaces, for a while. Then choose a footwork style that you can make work and perfect it. Continue to experiment afterwards to perfect smaller, larger, or more particular kinds of steps. Practicing crossing the line, straight footwork, and various angles at varying widths, can increase your options as a fighter. You will benefit most from such things when you build on a stable footwork style that you've already established as a foundation for yourself.

On the related subject of footwear all the *fechtbucher* I have read depict thin flat-soled shoes. Most of their shoes are essentially simple leather slippers. I suggest finding thin flat-soled shoes for training.

Theory: stepping and cutting

Ringeck's teachings on footwork and cutting consist only of a few lines regarding some essential principles. First, '*learn to strike all blows equally well from both sides*': you must learn in a balanced way, so that there will be no weakness in your style when you find you need to strike from your weaker side. If you do not do this then your technique will fall apart as soon as you reach the first permutations under pressure. Let me emphasize. Virtually every single technique in this book must be practiced thoroughly from both sides. For the purposes of conserving space I will not depict all such actions, and you must make the necessary adjustments yourself.

Second, strike as you step. If you do otherwise your body will not help propel your weapon or support the strike during contact. Thus, if you want to cut from your right, begin with the left foot forward, and step with the right foot as you cut, and vice versa. With practice this may be done stepping forward, backward, sideways, and with very simple footwork variations that do not involve changing which foot is in front. If you use simple or gathering steps you can shift your weight or the leg on which your weight rests to give you greater range of motion. Always let the strike fall so that the foot on the side the cut comes from lands well before, or well after, the sword reaches the target, so that the impact of your foot will not disturb your cut.

Some have argued that limiting oneself to such synchronized cutting and stepping is unnecessary, and, on occasion, impractical. I strongly disagree. Not only does all of Ringeck's iconography show synchronized footwork, but in my experience, when people step and cut asynchronously with longswords they are always compensating for a mistake. Some believe that it is necessary to learn this kind of footwork for situations that arise unintentionally. I argue that they never should have let themselves get into those situations in the first place, and that other actions that use synchronized footwork can fill the same roles without compromising your body's structure. Unsynchronized forms of footwork aren't inherently useful, or good methods that ought to be practiced and perfected. When people devote training time to them they are simply trying to make up for insufficient training in the prescribed footwork of the style, and I feel that that time would be better spent ingraining proper footwork and technique. With proper training in synchronized footwork you will always have a clean, strong, and tactically safe option that matches Ringeck's teachings.

While one can, with training, make good cuts with unsynchronized footwork, and while other weapon systems can make use of unsynchronized footwork, with longswords, using synchronized footwork supports your attacks and defenses with your entire body, and is always stronger. Your legs, hips, shoulders, and arms can all more easily support a blow with synchronized footwork. This also echoes Liechtenauer's later teaching to *'fight with all your strength,'* which can also been rendered *'fight with your entire body.'* So, while it is possible to do otherwise, and important to be aware of such possibilities, it is, as far as I can tell, always better to attempt to fight in such a way that you can do as Ringeck says.

Perhaps more importantly, in a historical European martial art we should be trying to achieve accuracy to the historical technique by exactly replicating the techniques as the ancient masters taught them, and figuring out why they did so. While the absolute language in Ringeck is often followed by exceptions this is not the case here. It is counterproductive to the accuracy of the interpretation to assume that a wholly different method ought to be adopted in regular practice because we have trouble living up to the standard set. Nor would it be appropriate to deal with the exceptions in depth from the beginning. If such things should be taught at all they should be left for after a strong foundation has been established in a student's habits.

Method: how to step

Unfortunately, Ringeck offers almost nothing on how to step or what kinds of steps to perform. I have found Joachim Meyer's teachings on the different kinds of steps very helpful for understanding how Ringeck may have taught his students, and I have loosely based the following stepping drills on Meyer's teachings, with an eye toward the iconography of the Glasgow manual. Meyer came at the very end of the active practice of the Liechtenauer tradition, and differs from the primary works of that tradition in many important respects. One such respect is posture. Meyer typically shows very forward-weighted postures leaning the torso deeply into the strikes, and most of the time he shows very extended arms. The older manuals tend to show more upright postures, which are only slightly forward-weighted and usually use straighter legs. They also more frequently show back-weighted stances. The older manuals also usually show somewhat smaller steps than Meyer, though there are notable exceptions. I feel that less extreme steps tend to work better with Ringeck's cutting technique because they can be done more quickly than larger steps. This allows you to line up your body and weapon more easily. In my opinion, the greater stability and control over your body more than compensates for the slightly shorter range produced by this footwork.

When going forwards, make sure that you make contact with the whole foot as it comes down so that you maximize the friction and grip you have on the ground. I advise my students to press into the ground and outward with the ball and heel of

We begin in our basic stance.

Make contact with the ball of the foot.

Press down with both the ball and heel on the inside of both feet. Shift weight so that it is balanced between the feet and press down and outward from the inside of both feet.

both their feet evenly. The ball of the foot should make contact slightly before the heel in all steps. If you aim your step to place you to the side of your opponent rather than going straight in, then the enemy will be forced to adjust to the new position, and this can increase the time it takes for them to defend against your attacks. If they are not quick enough you will hit them while they are vulnerable and less stable. Remember doing this requires obtaining a slightly closer distance, or using greater extension with your arms, than directly attacking. When the foot lands it should utilize as much of its surface area as possible with the weight focused on the inside surfaces of the feet. As students become more confident the back foot may be permitted to lift the heel from the ground in the *Zufechten*, which is consistent with iconography in manuals such as Paulus Hector Mair's, but not too much, nor too often, especially not in the early stages of training. This can help you gain a little more extension, or by beginning contraction of the muscles of the leg preparatory to a step make the step faster. Be aware, however, that doing this dramatically reduces the stability of your stance, and for this reason it is inappropriate once good distance has been reached.

Place your forward foot so that it points towards your opponent. If you step to the side you will need to pigeon-toe your new foot to some degree so that it points at the opponent. If you step across the center line this will result in a reverse L-shape when stepping with the right foot. Press down and outwards with your weight into the ball and heel of the foot. Be sure to align your knees with your feet when you step across the center line, and you may choose to bend your knees more than usual to settle your weight and project force downwards. This will help prevent rolling your ankle.

In all your stances keep your center of gravity suspended between your legs and at a height a little lower than when you normally walk so that you remain stable. This will give you greater control over where and how you can move your weight and increase the speed you can move it with. The space between the balls and heels of your feet form a trapezoid and if you keep your center of gravity within it you will remain balanced. If your center of gravity is moved outside of that area you will begin to fall.

Theory: starting positions

Ringeck does not explain the guards that people should strike from until after he teaches the five strikes. I believe this is intentional. The Liechtenauer tradition uses an aggressive and punishing fighting style that emphasizes seeing the opponent's openings, attacking them swiftly, and not giving them room to respond properly. We will, however, need a position to learn from. I suggest that *Vom Tag*, 'From the Roof,' or 'From the Day,' depending on the translation, is the best place to start because it requires less concentration for the beginners to maintain, is a natural fit for an offensive strategy, and it is easier to strike from both sides using this position.

Vom Tag is done by standing upright with the feet about shoulder-width apart, the forward foot pointing at the opponent, or slightly turned in, and the shoulders and hips facing the opponent, or slightly turned in. The Glasgow manual shows the sword being held with the hilt tucked very close to the armpit with the blade resting on the shoulder. Do not get lazy with this stance and let your sword rest lower on your side by the level of your belt. This robs the stance of most of the power it can generate. *Vom Tag* can also be done by raising the weapon above the head with the sword angled back and up. Kal shows the weapon essentially straight up, while Talhoffer and Paulus Hector Mair show it done on a roughly forty-five degree angle. Be sure when holding *Vom Tag* above the head that the arms do not drift forward, which makes them viable targets for attacks which would otherwise be out of reach.

One might, however, make a strong case for using *Ochs* as your starting position. Ringeck, and other masters of the Liechtenauer tradition, always mention *Ochs* first

This *Vom Tag* is drawn from Dobringer and Ringeck.

This *Vom Tag* replicates Paulus Kal's version.

This *Vom Tag* replicates the position seen in Paulus Hector Mair's *Fechtbook*.

This *Ochs* guard is drawn from Dobringer's *fechtbuch*.

This *Ochs* is drawn from the Glasgow version of Ringeck's *fechtbuch*. It is back weighted but side oriented so that the bent leg is the back leg even though both are relatively the same distance from the opponent. We show it here from the front and the side.

when they finally get around to introducing the guards, both in the section on guards, as well as when they introduce the other four strikes which are designed to break the four guards. This position feels safer to beginning students, and may allow them to focus better. It also presents a direct threat with the point which must be avoided to deliver strikes, and it covers one of the upper openings. This can help students develop non-linear footwork, and it will help new students see their opponent's openings more clearly.

Beginning in *Ochs*, however, makes cutting much slower as the weapon requires an additional 180 degrees of rotation in order to make a good cut. This can breed a false sense of the speed of good cuts, and provide a tell they may grow over-accustomed to when training. In addition, for large

This *Ochs* is drawn from the Goliath *fechtbuch*.

classes, the unique limitations of the guard, the fact that it is set up to thrust, and its asymmetrical nature will become difficult, and raise numerous questions and concerns as the students adjust to this less-intuitive position.

For simplicity's sake I will assume you will use *Vom Tag* for the rest of this book, and that the fighters are right-handed. Remember, all attacks should be learned equally well from both sides anyways. Practice all of the steps going forward, to each side, and backward. If you are left-handed you will use the same foot forward and backward, and cut from the same side as it is explained in the drills. Always practice all drills from both sides.

Bear in mind that every technique and variation from here on out will, eventually, need to be practiced with all the different kinds of footwork. This will vastly multiply the number of times that you drill particular techniques, and help you apply them intuitively in the widest possible variety of circumstances.

Tips for teachers: dedicated footwork with drills

I do not spend a great deal of time teaching footwork through footwork drills. I prefer to teach it during regular drills where the emphasis is on what you are achieving with your sword and helping the students see and understand how to use their footwork within the context of each technique. Nevertheless, it is important to be able to isolate and practice these actions, and from time to time I will have a student practice a particular stance or sequence of steps for an extended time. The feet should stay very close to the ground, hovering just above it during stepping as this tends to make the stance more stable and makes it easier to adjust to new situations because you can feel changes in the ground beneath your feet. After practicing a step practice striking with it. Always synchronize the feet with the sword.

Theory: balancing your weight

Most martial arts show a distinct preference for a specific stance. The only illustrated version of Ringeck's manual shows many types of stances, some holding the weight forward, a few with the weight back, and a couple in laterally oriented back-weighted positions, but the majority of the stances depicted show a fairly standard forward stance with relatively wide footwork. If we compare this with the other books in the Liechtenauer tradition we find that Ringeck is pretty consistent in his ratios and where these stances occur. One notable exception within the tradition is Paulus Kal, who uses a balanced stance with very straight legs for the vast majority of his plays and only uses a forward stance a few times. He might not even use any back-weighted stances at all, depending on how you interpret his images. The underlying reason for the prevalence of the forward stance in the Liechtenauer tradition seems to be that Liechtenauer and students taught a very aggressive style, and the forward attacking motions of the weapon are usually best supported by a forward-weighted stance.

Method: forward stances

Stand with your hips and shoulders facing squarely at, or only slightly turned off to the side, from your target. The foot of your sword-arm side should be back about your shoulder's width laterally from your other foot, or a little farther, positioned well back and turned out. Press downward and out with both feet. Do this with all your stances. Practice stepping into this position, from both sides. The stance should have about 60% of your weight supported by your forward foot. We occasionally see the knee move a little past the heel in later sources, but, especially in the older manuals, never past the toes. Most depictions contemporary with Ringeck show the heel below or in front of the knee rather than behind.

This forward stance comes from the Glasgow manual, the oldest illustrated version of Ringeck.

Tilt your head slightly back and keep your eyes focused at the center of your opponent's body. You will notice a lot of extra light coming into your eyes, and that this head position extends your peripheral vision by a few degrees. This head position comes from my examination of the head positions of the figures in German manuals, which very often show the head cocked back a few degrees, or sometimes much more. It is consistent throughout the stances in the German sources which we are trying to emulate here.

Method: back-weighted stances

Hanko Dobringer's depiction of *Ochs* shows a back-weighted stance. In the I.33 back-weighted stances seem to be the primary kind of opening position. Several other manuals show transitional positions in the bind which are back-weighted. In Dobringer the head is tilted backwards, which improves peripheral vision. This

This image replicates Dobringer's depiction of *Ochs*.

This image replicates an example of Sigmund Ringeck's side oriented back weighted stance from the Glasgow Manual. It is shown from the front, rather than from the side as it is depicted in that book.

position does not appear frequently in the iconography, and only very infrequently after the engagement begins, but it can allow you to obtain an advantageous range, and give you a more explosive initial step. It can sometimes expose your forward leg as a target, so be careful of that. Be careful not to let your weight drift too far back or you will lose the capacity to go forward.

Sigmund Ringeck has a particularly useful form of back-weighted stance which he orients to the side. This can be extremely useful at generating power as the fight begins, and helps move you into an advantageous position to the side as well as forward.

Method: balanced stance

We see this especially in Paulus Kal where the legs are relatively straight and the body is situated upright between them. This position doesn't usually lend itself to large footwork such as that shown in Talhoffer or Meyer, but is very quick with small footwork, and in all directions. Its higher center of gravity makes it somewhat less stable up close, but this can be easily adjusted for.

Paulus Kal makes extensive use of the balanced stance and uses almost exclusively straight legs.

Method: the passing step

This step forms the literal foundation of this fighting style. Learn it thoroughly. First, stand with the legs slightly bent to lower your center of gravity, so that both legs can exert leverage on your center and let you move in the widest possible set of directions. In most circumstances, when you do this properly, your head and center of gravity will remain at a consistent height, and not bob up and down, the way most peoples' do when they walk. Please understand that maintaining a certain height is a symptom of good footwork, not the desired result, and that sometimes

raising and lowering your center of gravity can and should be done to succeed in a particular technique. We are trying to avoid the long periods in normal walking when a person has only one point of contact with the ground and cannot control the direction and motion of their body.

Instruct your group to keep their eyes up, and make sure that they step slightly offline and turn towards the opponent with their new forward side. They will need to pigeon-toe the foot they step with when they step offline. The foot which begins forward will need to adjust with a rotating motion to support the new stance. This is usually accomplished by pressing into the ball of your foot, while the heel rotates around it. Sometimes you may need to make a very small second step with your new back foot to stabilize your new position, particularly after a large step. Simply reverse this process going backwards, and remember that the ball of your foot should always land first.

Method: the passing step and cut

Now we will practice stepping with a *Zornhau*. The cut should begin at the side of the back foot and end at the side of the new back foot. Aim these at targets about ear height with good control and stable stepping. Do not attempt to go fast. Focus on getting the motion correct and remaining synchronized. Make sure everyone focuses their eyes up at a target that they 'cut' through.

Method: the simple step

This step is not explicitly covered in the teachings of Ringeck, but is covered in Meyer's writings and I believe it is essential for small distance adjustments. I argue that it will in fact be a valid inclusion in an interpretation of Ringeck, as long as the feet remain synchronized with the sword. One executes this step by pushing off the back foot, and stepping with the front foot and then bringing the back foot up behind it to a normal width. When entering good striking distance, aim the step to move yourself slightly off to the side of a target with a slight pigeon-toeing in the first step, and turn so that you square your stance with the opponent as the back foot follows. When moving backwards begin with the back foot and let the front foot follow. Again, reverse this to go backwards.

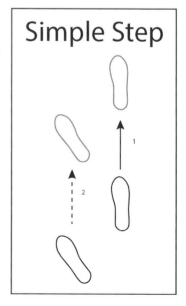

Simple Step

Method: simple step sideways

Take your stance and push your body sideways with either leg. Land with the foot leading the action then bring the foot you pushed off of into place to stabilize you. As always reverse this to go the other direction.

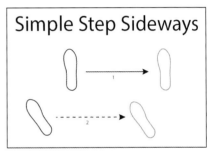

Method: the gathering step

The gathering step provides a very clever way to manipulate distance. It allows us to make much bigger steps than a regular simple step, including large lunges. Execute the gathering step by bringing the back foot forward until it is close to the front foot, press down and into the back foot, then use the back foot's new position to begin a regular simple step, or a large lunging simple step, with the front foot. Remember to step ball-heel, and keep your balance solid at all times. Begin small, after some practice move on to bigger steps. Again, make sure you practice stepping on angles, as well as sideways and backwards.

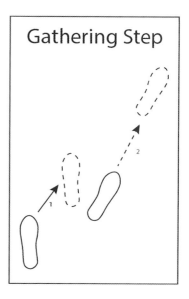

Method: gathering step and cut

Practice delivering strikes with a gathering step, forwards, backwards and laterally. Remember to keep the head angled up, focus on a target and strike through it while synchronizing the motion of the sword and feet.

Method: about face – *Vom Tag* to *Ochs*

This kind of action provides the fastest way to reverse direction. You press into the balls of your feet and rotate your body toward your rear foot then settle in the new guard. Stand in *Vom Tag* with your sword extending up and back from over your shoulder or over your head. Let the point of your sword drop as you swivel your body until it is aimed at your new target's face in an *Ochs* guard. Now do the same thing in reverse and you will find yourself in *Vom Tag*. There are many ways to transition from various guards into other positions in this manner. This is provided as the chief example as these will be the guards that feature prominently in the scope of this work.

Method: about face and strike

Begin in *Ochs*, execute the about face, take a passing step in forward or backward in the new direction that you are facing and execute a *Zornhau*. You can go from *Vom Tag* to *Ochs* and thrust as well.

Method: turning step

This step gives you a way to change your direction while roughly maintaining your current position. Simply take one of your feet, usually your back foot, step behind your other foot to a comfortable distance and rotate your body at the hips while maintaining pressure on the ball of your stationary foot to align your front heel properly with your desired direction. This can also be done stepping around toward the front with the rear foot.

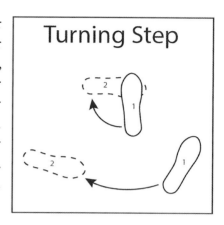

Method: passing step across the line

This technique requires two actions in quick succession. It allows you to move in the opposite direction of many kinds of steps and can give you better positions. In your basic stance, starting with the left foot forward, step forward to the left side of your left foot with your right foot, place the ball of your foot on the ground pressing outwards with both the ball and heel as you settle the whole foot down. Make sure your foot is pointed at your opponent. Your legs will need to flex according to the needs of your new position. Open your hips and aim the knees and toes of your back foot outward to the rear to enlarge the space your center of gravity rests in and bend your knees so your weight sinks into the strike.

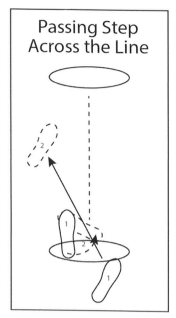

Passing Step Across the Line

Tips for teachers: all arts have length and measure

I spend a great deal of time running my students through the following drills. The single easiest mistake to exploit is attacking from too far away. It allows any number of very simple *Nachreissen* (chasing/pursuit) which can instantly end a fight. Return to these very simple drills from time to time. Attacking in proper distance prevents these techniques, keeps the hands from becoming vulnerable, and makes one's attacks more effective.

Theory: approach with the left foot, and cut with the right

Liechtenauer and Ringeck explicitly state that, if we are right-handed, we should enter good distance with our left foot, and then strike as we step with our right foot. Likewise, if we are left-handed, we should approach so that we enter good distance with our right foot forward and strike while stepping with our left foot. Students should approach their opponent with passing steps, and as they reach good distance they should adjust which foot they have forward, if necessary, so that they can step and strike with the desired foot.

Drill: finding range

This drill will begin teaching the student how to recognize when they have entered good distance. The original manuals refer to the opening phase of a fight when the opponents approach each other as *Zufechten*. The partners should always begin every drill well out of distance so that they constantly practice entering good distance. This is the first proper partner drill, so I will explain the proceedure for it here. The participant who is in the role of the student will be the attacker, and the one filling the role of the teacher will be the defender. The student says 'Draw' when they are ready, and the teacher says 'Attack' when they are ready. The attacker advances with any footwork they deem necessary, and then, when they believe they are close enough to start their attack, they extend their sword, without stepping, to see if they can reach the target with the correct portion of the blade. If they can, then they should then carefully execute their cut with a step.

This exercise requires our attacker, Ben, to take multiple steps to approach his opponent. He must learn when he can able to strike effectively, and when he cannot. Beginning well out of distance ensures the student masters length and measure, and accustoms themselves to approaching a dangerous opponent, which is crucial for Ringeck's style.

Here we see Ben reaching out with his sword without having taken a step in order to check if he has entered good distance.

Notice the final position incorporates comfortable extension, lateral motion in the passing step and strong coordination of the legs, hips, shoulders and arms.

Drill: calibrating control

In this drill the attacker will learn how fast they can strike safely, and practice using the highest level of speed they safely can. The defender's job is to control the instinct to flinch. Have pairs of students practice the previous drill, but this time the attacker should attempt to strike as quickly as they safely can. The weapon should stop in a position that demonstrates that they could have struck the defender a debilitating blow. They should increase their levels of speed and force while maintaining safety. Emphasize that this is an exercise in control. The weapon should be stopped with no contact. Occasional light contact is acceptable, but it should not be a regular occurrence, and anything beyond light contact should earn a swift reprimand. The defender may use their own weapon to make a simple static block if they feel it absolutely necessary.

Drill: finding range with a moving target

Continue as above, but the defender should now be a moving target and attempt to avoid getting hit by stepping out of the attacker's strike or stepping in to grab their arms. Again make sure that 4–8in of the blade extends past the point of contact. The intent of this drill is to teach the students to understand length and measure in a dynamic situation.

Tips for teachers: Forward motion and blade impact

Remember, if the sword moves before the feet, then significant forward motion may take place after the moment of contact in a real fight. Be on the lookout for students misreading the distance, and correct it immediately by advising the student that they must move closer to their opponent before they can attack effectively. Watch for this throughout this stage of a student's training.

Lesson 3: Fighting with a Longsword

The Text of Another Lesson
He who moves after his strikes will find little joy in his art.
Close with your foe when you cut so you can work your will, and prevent Durchwechseln from penetrating your shield.[27]
Throw swift strikes to the head and the body.
When you choose to fight, fight with all your strength.

Gloss – When you prepare to fight, do not watch his cuts or wait for what he will try against you. All fighters who wait for their opponent's strikes, and do nothing but defend, will have no joy from this art, because they will very often be struck.

When you fight always use all your strength. As you come at him aim for his head and body. Close with him so that he cannot change through with his point in front of you. If you bind with him strike swiftly to the nearest opening, which shall be explained hereafter in the sections on the five cuts and other techniques. (The Dresden Manuscript)

Theory: the sword as your shield

In longsword fighting you use both hands on a single weapon. It is your shield. A longsword can only effectively protect one quarter at a time, so you must position it carefully. In most exchanges the weapons will meet, and this meeting is called a bind. Our goal, when defending, will be to become strong when the swords bind. This forces the opponent to attempt to change the position in their favor before they can attack. Our attacks must be delivered in a way that cannot be easily dominated by our opponent. If the point of maximum extension in your strike leaves your sword

Ben has struck his *Zornort* so that his sword rests on the left side of his body creating significant space between himself and Randy's weapon.

dead center in front of you, you will leave both sides of your body unprotected. So, when you strike, you should not extend your whole sword to a point dead center in front of you, but the strong and hilt should move off to the side you are striking towards, to cover your most vulnerable quarter. This should place the sword right where Ringeck indicated in the previous lesson, 'in front of the left foot' when you strike from your right.

To ensure your defenses give you the best protection possible, always use the correct distance for the defense you have chosen. Ringeck taught 'Close with your foe when you cut so you can work your will' which I interpret as moving close enough to strike with 4-8in of your blade past your target without needing to step. We should of course step, but at this distance our step will accelerate the action, rather than force us to match the speed of our cut to our step. At the distance Ringeck seems to be teaching us to fight at knowledge and training matters far more than muscle, reach, or other physical advantages. This also has the effect of limiting the possibility of *Durchwechseln*, one of the swiftest, and most deadly maneuvers. *Durchwechseln* can instantly exploit an opening if you fail to threaten your opponent. At the distance I interpret Ringeck instructing us to fight at this becomes very difficult, and requires much bigger mistakes to leave yourself open to *Durchwechseln*.

Theory: fight with all your strength

I believe Liechtenauer's and Ringeck's command to '*fight with all you strength*' has a double meaning. First, it carries with it an implicit warning to always take all fencing seriously and never become overconfident, or believe you can easily beat an opponent. Second, when your body mechanics are working correctly every part of your body contributes to your strike: the movement of your feet, the turn of your hips and torso, your shoulder, chest, and back muscles, as well as your arms and hands should all contribute to your strike's power, accuracy, and leverage.

Theory: avoiding *Durchwechseln* and *Nachreissen*

Ringeck teaches quite clearly that striking to the head and body at the correct distance prevents an opponent from using a *Durchwechseln* 'change through' against you. If you strike too high to threaten your opponent with your point he will *Durchwechseln* and kill you. If, on the other hand, you strike too low when you aim at the upper quarters, you risk being weak in the bind. If you begin a fight with a strike to the lower quarters, which include the hips, legs and the lower part of the belly, your range will be significantly reduced and your opponent may use *Nachreissen*, a free strike at an exposed quarter. If you strike at the head and body, and always maintain a threat, your opponent will have to bind and remain at the sword where you will have some control over what happens, and more importantly you will be able to feel his position and intent.

Tips for teachers: throw swift strikes to the head and the body

Demonstrate a *Durchwechseln* 'change through' to your students by moving your point under a sword that is extended, but that does not threaten you, and thrusting to the exposed opening. You should inform the group that as the lessons progress if their partner strikes too high in their *Zornhau* they should be stopped and corrected because of this. Eventually, once you have reached the Durchwechseln 'change through' section which I will cover in future volumes, you will want to give the group permission to do it when their fellow group members commit this egregious error. Aim your attacks at the head and the body, or you leave yourself open to these techniques. The converse logic is worth noting here as it justifies Ringeck. This sort of technique can only be done to exploit a particular mistake, and if you maintain a

Here we see a classic aiming of a *Zornhau* squarely at the ear.

Here we see a *Zornhau* aimed between the eyes. This targeting only appears in later manuals from other traditions, but is the theoretical upper limit of the angling of this strike.

Here we see how moving the strike just a few inches higher leads to a complete miss. The proximity of the strike to the head leads most new fighters to react unnecessarily.

Here Ben sees that Randy's parry is too high, and he can see the underside of his blade. He decides to execute a *Durchwechseln*.

Ben lowers his body and withdraws his sword letting Randy's sword pass by and prepares to thrust.

Ben thrusts his blade to Randy's head completing the technique. The thrust can also be done from an *Ochs* position on either side, or aimed at the chest if necessary.

constant threat while fighting from correct distance you will remove the threat of *Durchwechseln*, because it will become suicidal to disengage from your weapon while there is an imminent threat of a cut or thrust. Ringeck's logic in showing this here is to prevent the student from facing this deadly technique by teaching them a style that allows them to prevent offering the opening that *Durchwechseln* exploits, not so that they learn it now.

Theory: the Glasgow *Durchwechseln*

There are several simple ways to do *Durchwechseln*, but there is a unique, and particularly useful variation that appears in the Glasgow version of Ringeck's book. Folio 15v of the Glasgow manual is the only place in Ringeck's manuals that provides an illustration of *Durchwechseln*, though several other techniques include it as an option. The illustrator depicts it with the left hand in a reverse grip, and the point low toward the ground mid action. I believe the angle of the sword may be an exaggeration due to the mode of art of the time and the skill of the artist, but the technique is sound.

Do it this way: when you see an opportunity to *Durchwechseln*, begin to wind to your left, moving your weapon's point down as needful. Release the grip of the left hand, but maintain contact with the palm on the pommel, turn the hand to the other side of the pommel and grip the handle again, just below the pommel in reverse so that the knuckles are up and the fingers are on the same side as our sword hand's fingers. Use the pressure of the left hand to move the point rapidly in a large circle around the opponent's sword so that you can plant a clean thrust to

Here Ben sees that Randy's parry is too wide to threaten him, but Randy is rather closer, and his sword is a little lower, than it was before. He decides to execute a *Durchwechseln* in the style of the Glasgow manual.

the upper or lower quarters on the other side as convenient. It takes less practice than you might think to execute the grip change well, and then to be able to leave it quickly for follow up techniques. Because of the position, and its placement in the manual, I interpret its appearance in the Glasgow illustration as being executed against bad lateral parry, rather than against a cut as shown in the previous sequence. It works perfectly well though in every situation where a *Durchwechseln* is justified. It allows you to cover other quarters left vulnerable by other variations of the technique. Because of the additional leverage, the point can move on a wider arc without sacrificing as much speed as you normally would to do the technique.[28]

Ben guides his point through a wide circle around Randy's longsword by opening his off-hand and reversing his grip.

Ben ends the *Durchwechseln* in an Ochs guard on his right side with the point aimed at Randy's face.

Lesson 4: Fighting from the Left and Right

And Another Lesson
   Hear what is bad: do not fight above the left if you are right-handed, and if you are left-handed on the right you will be weak.

Note: There are two kinds of people, the left-handed and the right-handed. If you are right-handed and you close with an opponent and you see that you can hit him, do not strike the first blow from your left side. Because you will be weak there and you cannot withstand him if he binds strongly. So cut from the right side and you will be strong at the sword and can use all the techniques you like.
   It is the same if you are left-handed, do not cut from the right side. Fighting with skill is difficult if you are left-handed and use a technique from the right, and the same is true of a right-hander from the left. (The Dresden Manuscript)

Method: fighting from the left and right

These principles will chiefly affect your footwork, measure, and leverage. To follow Ringeck's instruction you may need to use a combination of passing, simple, and gathering steps as you approach an opponent so that your strong side is ready when you get to the appropriate range to attack. This way you can pass forward when you reach the appropriate range and strike from your strong side. You can start with your strong side back and use gathering and simple steps to enter range when you reach the edge of your opponent's reach, or you can use passing steps or even a run, and vary it at the second to last step with a simple or gathering step if you need to. Gauging the distance and choosing the proper footwork for different kinds of approaches takes practice. If an opponent tries to aggresively close the distance it can become necessary to take a passing step backwards from an approach to bring your strong side forward into the strike.

   When fighting a person who is opposite-handed the advantage of being the one to strike from their strong side becomes even greater, as is the weakness of being forced to do otherwise. Being right-handed or left-handed does not change your tactical choices when fighting another person with a longsword within Ringeck and Liechtenauer's system of combat, it just makes the results more distinctly good or bad when you execute them. Also remember, that Ringeck first told us to learn to strike all blows equally well on both sides, so make sure to split your training time relatively equally.

Lesson 5: *Vor* and *Nach*

This is the Text of the Lesson about Vor *and* Nach

Vor and Nach, from these two things
All skill springs.
Weak and Strong
In the Moment, mark those words
Thus, you will learn
To work and defend with skill.
If you easily take fright,
Then you should not learn to fight.

Gloss – Before all other things you must understand Vor and Nach very well, and from these two things emerge the entire art of fighting. The first is Vor. Which is when you make a cut or a thrust to his opening, and force him to defend. Then work nimbly from their defense with your sword from one opening to another, and he will not be able to use his own techniques. If he closes with you, grapple with him. (The Dresden Manuscript)

Theory: translating *Vor* and *Nach*

While literally *Vor* means 'before' and *Nach* means 'after,' these words do not express the meaning that Liechtenauer and Ringeck are trying to convey. Many people use the word 'initiative' in place of *Vor*, and it is a decent substitute, but the meaning of the word *Vor* has some subtleties in this particular context that the word initiative does not convey. *Vor*, in this context, means something closer to '*being free to attack*.' *Nach* means precisely the opposite: one is '*not free to attack*,' or in other words, their opponent is giving them a clear threat that they must deal with before they can attack safely. These two words offer succinct shortcuts to these more complex ideas and I suggest using them directly instead of English substitutes.

Theory: *Vor* and *Nach*

These words give expression to one of the core ideas of the Liechtenauer tradition's fighting philosophy. Sword fights happen in a fairly predictable pattern. The person who executes a correct technique against an opponent's vulnerable opening while maintaining their own defenses wins. Performing poor technique usually doesn't defeat anyone, except by chance. Good techniques still need openings to exploit, and this usually only happens when an opponent makes a mistake. Among new fighters the first person to execute a good technique generally wins. Among very experienced fighters the first person to make a mistake loses. The masters of the Liechtenauer tradition advise students to seize the *Vor*, to be offensive in their fighting strategy. Attacking gives you an opportunity to win, and the more often you attack the more likely you will get through their defenses and win.

The reverse also holds true. If you allowed your opponent to seize the *Vor*, and you find yourself needing to defend your openings, Ringeck and the other masters of this style teach to seek the most efficient way to defend so that you can immediately regain the ability to safely attack, ideally with the same action that you use to defend. This is the *Nach*.

Ben has wound his sword to defend himself and seize the *Vor*. Randy must now respond or be struck.

Tips for teachers: *Vor* and *Nach*

Demonstrations often help students quickly comprehend this principle. With an assistant, begin well out of distance. Ask 'Who has the *Vor*?'' The answer is no one. You should approach to close distance and ask 'Who has the *Vor*?' again. The answer will depend on who entered distance and how they did so. Was it straight in, was it with a step on the side of the opponent, did someone blink, etc... Changes to the exact situation will affect who has the *Vor* when you enter close distance. Then demonstrate an *Oberhau*. The defender should not move but let the blow make gentle contact, and ask again 'Who has the *Vor*?' Explain that an opponent must defend to avoid being killed. Now have the defender execute the *Zornort*, and ask again 'Who has the *Vor*?' Continue through the different stages of the *Zornhau* drill, and other techniques, to get them used to establishing who has the *Vor* at each moment by pointing out who is threatened and how.

In a different demonstration move to the edge of good distance and ask 'Who has the *Vor*?' The answer here is complicated because at this particular range an attack can be ineffective and easy to read, so while one can attack from extreme range in practice the person who is technically 'defending' may, in fact, have the *Vor* because they might be able to confidently read the move and execute the perfect defense, leaving no time for the attacker to adjust or respond to it. It can be helpful to examine other techniques besides the *Zornhau* and its permutations with the class as well.

For example, in the case of two persons who approach in right *Pflug* the answer is that neither of them has the Vor. If either tries a direct attack they are still exposed to the opponent's attack. Now have the attacker move to left *Pflug* and set the defender's point aside as they thrust. Establish with the students that because he has cut off his opponent's line of attack the attacker gains the safety to attack. Continue with permutations in many different situations, including those that are mid-action, constantly asking the students 'Who is free to attack?' A couple of sparring matches will be helpful to show how this works in practice. Once your students begin sparring and you are reviewing their bouts start asking them questions about who had the *Vor* and when and how they gained and lost it.

Ben and Randy begin from well out of distance. Neither will have the *Vor* until they close with their opponent. Whoever enters the space their opponent can reach will be in the *Nach* unless their opponent hesitates.

Here Ben is measuring his reach and finds he cannot strike without taking a step forward. While he could potentially hit Randy by stepping while he strikes, this will drastically increase the time Randy has to react and make it difficult for him to succeed. Attacking at this distance can yield the *Vor* to Randy.

Here Randy has seized the *Vor* by successfully executing a winding against a thrust at his lower quarter. Ben must wind beneath with a special *Durchwechseln*, or cut to another opening with *Abnemen* to retake the *Vor*.

Theory: if he closes with you

Ringeck's advice at the end of this section, to grapple with an opponent who runs in at you, presumes knowledge of wrestling. While the eight *Durchlauffen* near the end of the manual, the two grappling techniques in the *Zwerchhau* section, and the half-sword throw in the section on *Versetzen*, give us an excellent set of techniques for grappling at the sword, Ringeck has not yet shared any of these here. While it would be ideal for all our students to have a background in a grappling art, such is usually not the case in the modern world. Grappling systems are complex arts unto themselves. They take months or years to learn well. These circumstances force us to choose either: a) offer only demonstrations and limited instruction on one or two moves, relying on this and the hand slice instruction in the *Zornhau* section to suffice, and press on through Ringeck's techniques till we get to the lessons on grappling, or b) stop and spend considerable time teaching some common defensive grappling moves, breaking the order in which the material is taught. I usually choose a), and reserve grappling instruction for when grappling techniques are actually taught in the manual.

Grappling techniques require more complex movement, take more time, and are usually less immediately devastating than cuts, thrusts, or slices. I believe the structure of Ringeck's book, using a very small number of moves at later places in the manual, de-prioritizes them. I, therefore, interpret wrestling in this style as a last resort to be employed only after the sword work, hand slices, and distance management have failed. I will, however, demonstrate several strikes, grips, and throws for my students so that they understand that this can happen, and what they can do about it. I'll include just one example here.

Ben and Randy bind at a particularly close distance. Ben is weak in the bind and decides he would prefer a closing strategy in this situation.

Ben decides to execute a pommel strike to Randy's face, setting his point aside in the process.

Randy deflects the pommel strike with his forearm.

Randy steps between Ben's feet, using his right thigh and hip to disturb Ben's balance, and wraps his arm around Ben's back, setting him up for a hip throw.

Randy executes the throw.

Tips for teachers: if he closes with you

In my experience good grappling distance should be measured the same way good sword distance is. If you can seize your opponent in the way you want to, without moving your feet, then you are in good distance to do that technique. If you are farther away than that, then you should use other techniques. Demonstrate a few basic wrestling techniques, and include the actions of the sword, such as hand slices, and half-swording. The goal of this is not to teach the students to do this yet, but to match Ringeck's pattern of exposing a student to advanced techniques so they will gain some understanding of what they are learning to counter, and how best to prevent it. Remember the best counter to an attempted grapple is controlling the distance of a fight. If an opponent cannot get close enough to grapple, then you will never have to worry about those techniques in the first place. Ringeck teaches hand slices as a more convenient, and often more devastating, counter should the opponent manage to close the distance effectively.

Ideally, your students should have some background in wrestling and unarmed combat. I strongly recommend training in unarmed fighting arts in conjunction with your sword work. Arts that work actively with and against weaponry are especially valuable. HEMA dagger and wrestling techniques are particularly well suited to prepare students for wrestling at the sword. Remember, at this point in the curriculum you are not trying to teach your students how to attack with these techniques, you are simply opening their minds to the possibilities.

Lesson 6: *Nach*

Here mark the Nach

   Mark, that if you cannot come at him with the Vor then wait for the Nach. Breaking every technique he tries to use against you. When he comes in the Vor then you must defend. From your defense, you must nimbly work Indes to his nearest opening. Thus, you will succeed before he can complete his technique. Thus, you will take the Vor, and he will remain in the Nach. Whether you are in the Vor, or the Nach, you must always think Indes, and perceive how you can work against the strong or weak of his sword. (The Dresden Manuscript)

Tips for teachers: the *Nach*

Explain to your students that *Nach* is when you are threatened and must defend. When you must defend you should strike immediately from the bind. Every defense should threaten your opponent and win you back the *Vor*. Emphasize that not choosing to attack with your defense is choosing to give your opponent another opportunity to threaten you. Consciously choose to defend to keep your mind clear. When you defend use the strong of the sword to meet the opponent's weak. Review the last paragraph of this section of the text. Demonstrate how one can hold opposed and how the leverage of the position dominates the situation rather than either opponent's muscle or size. Also demonstrate an ineffective defense aimed at

Here we see Randy make a bad parry, deflecting Ben's sword without hurting him, but they are too close for *Durchwechseln*.

Ben senses that he still has the *Vor* and begins to execute *Abnemen*.

the weapon rather than the person and how it fails to win you the *Vor*. The time involved in transitions from *Vor* to *Nach* and back again can be mere fractions of a second, and a single mistake in trading the *Vor* and *Nach* back and forth can leave the *Vor* in the hands of the opponent and let them strike you. What technique you should use to exploit this error depends on the distance and positions you and your opponent have.

Tips for teachers: *Indes*

Ben completes the *Abnemen*.

The moment you or your opponent begins an attack you have begun to work in what Liechtenauer and Ringeck call 'Indes'. The translation I prefer for *Indes* is 'in the moment.' Demonstrate that when the attack and defense meet there will be a bind. *Indes* is the time during which you must decide on your next action based on the input from your senses of sight and touch. Emphasize that feeling is the superior of the two senses for this kind of decision, but that sight plays an important role before the weapons touch and if a participant leaves the bind.

From any bind there will be at least one good choice. What you should choose depends on if you are weak or strong, and the precise positions of yourself and

In this image it is hard to tell from the outside who is weak and who is strong, but the fighters should be able to tell immediately by sensing the way the bind feels with their hands.

your opponent. From any bind the options might be to thrust directly as in the *Zornort*, to wind and thrust to the face or chest, wind and thrust low (*Mutieren*), cut to the next opening, slice to the head (*Duplieren*), slice the hands (*Abschneiden* or *Hend Drucken*), close to grapple (*Durchlaufen*), change through (*Durchwechseln*), or withdraw. The last one is only taught in Ringeck under one circumstance in the *Zwerchhau* section. I believe Ringeck did this because withdrawing cannot, by definition, win a fight, and often only forestalls the inevitable, especially against an aggressive and skilled opponent. Demonstrate for your students how these different options work at the strong or weak of your opponent's sword, and how the goal is to keep yourself safe with your strong while threatening with your weak.

Sword-fighting in close as Ringeck suggests happens too fast for the eyes to track easily, and much too fast for the cognitive brain to analyze and plan for while you are fighting. You must fight *Indes* 'in the moment,' relying on your training, and your instincts, so you can respond to your opponent's actions in time to break their techniques. You must practice intensive drills and sparring in order to develop the sensitivity and intuition necessary in order to read your opponent, and particularly their actions through contact with their blade. This way the moment your weapon touches theirs you know what to do.

Lesson 7: Strong and Weak

The strong of the sword extends from the cross to the center of the blade. With the strong you can effectively resist your opponent when he binds against you. The weak extends from the center of the blade to the point, if you bind with an opponent here you will not be able to resist your opponent when he binds against you. When you deeply understand this you can work skillfully to protect yourself. (The Dresden Manuscript)

Tips for teachers: strong and weak

In order for a *Zornort* to work properly it must place the strong of your blade on the weak of their blade, or at least on a portion that is weaker than yours. Many students will engage strong to strong, or middle to middle. This makes the technique less effective. It can be further muddled if the students do not execute committed strikes and instead press and resist sideways or up during the engagement. Uncommitted strikes and defenses aimed at the weapon can be easily dealt with by using *Durchwechseln* and other techniques, but these techniques are taught much later in the manual because they require finely tuned feeling of the bind, which new students will not have acquired yet.

Here Ben has bound on top of Randy's weak with the strong of his sword and is using his leverage advantage to attempt a thrust. No amount of direct force or effort will allow Randy to dominate the bind. In order to become strong in the bind and win the *Vor*, Randy must move his sword so that he is bound on another location with different leverage.

Lesson 8: Courage

Princes and gentlemen learn this same art so that they may stand among the very best, in earnest and in play, but if you are frightened easily then you should not learn the art of fighting. If your heart despairs, you will be beaten by anyone, no matter their skill. (The Dresden manuscript)

Tips for teachers: teaching courage

It is hard to say for certain how well courage can be learned. Certainly we can say that trained people tend to panic less often, but the real test of courage happens just before the action begins for real, in the decision whether or not and when to engage the opponent. In my experience someone who has a problem with fear will not take the offensive. They will fail to seek the *Vor*, and only defend against their opponent's blows until they are struck down, unless they are very, very, lucky. If you find a student with this problem, teaching them can prove very difficult. We modern practitioners have the luxury of not needing to send them away as unsuitable if we do not wish to, but it takes a major personal change to overcome deep-seated fear. All we can do is be realistic and honest, and hope they continue until they develop the capacity to face their fears.

This tendency particularly leads new students to leave themselves vulnerable to *Durchwechseln*. They will fight the sword instead of the person. The most important thing to do is to focus on showing them the consequences of the mistake by using techniques that exploit their mistakes against them and telling them how and why you did it. I have found training them to attack powerfully, with intent, over and over again, to be the best remedy to this problem. You may need to work them up to strong defenses by not responding at first and then increasing your resistance slowly. Practice will help with this a great deal, but it takes time and people often plateau for a while before they overcome this fundamental problem.

Lesson 9: Liechtenauer's Techniques

Here is the text of the five cuts
Learn five cuts from the right-hand side
And with them you will
Earn praise with your skill

Mark, these teachings show five secret cuts, which masters of the sword know never to speak of. You should defend with only these cuts when he attacks you from his right side. Look for which of the five cuts suits his first attack. Whoever can counter you without injury earns the praise of the master of these teachings, and is more skilled in this art than others who cannot fence against the five strikes. And you will find how you shall do these five strikes in the following writings. (The Dresden Manuscript)

This is the list of the Recital's techniques:
Zornhau, Krumphau, Zwerchhau,
Schilhau and Scheitelhau,
Alber, Versetzen,
Nachraisen,
Uberlauffen, cutting, and parrying,
Durchwechseln, Zucken,
Durchlaufen, Abschneiden,
Hande Drucken, Hangen,
Strike, Catching Sweeps, Stabbing and Thrusting

Gloss: Here we find named the rightful techniques of the art of the longsword. Their names are chosen to help you understand them. There are seventeen and they begin with the five strikes:

*The first is the Strike of Wrath (*Zornhau*)*
*The second is the Crooked Strike (*Krumphau*)*
*The third is the Crossing Strike (*Zwerchhau*)*
*The fourth is the Squinting Strike (*Schielhau*)*
*The fifth is the Vertex Strike (*Scheitelhau*)*
*The sixth is the Four Guards (*Vier Leger*)*
*The seventh is the Four Breaks (*Vier Versetzen*)*
*The eighth is Pursuing (*Nachraisen*)*
*The ninth is the Running Over (*Uberlauffen*)*
*The tenth Setting Aside (*Absetzen*)*

*The eleventh is Changing Through (*Durchwechseln*)*
*The twelfth is Twitching (*Zucken*)*
*The thirteenth is the Running Through (*Durchlauffen*)*
*The fourteenth is the Slicing Off (*Abschneiden*)*
*The fifteenth is Pressing the Hands (*Hend Drucken*)*
*The sixteenth is the Hangings (*Der Hengen*)*
*The seventeenth is the Windings (*Der Winden*)*

How you shall hang and wind to seek the openings, and how to execute the techniques named above, you shall find written hereafter.

Tips for teachers: teaching the strategy of Ringeck

The goal of learning this fighting style is to learn to fight from a foundation of the five strikes: the *Zornhau*, *Krumphau*, *Zwerchhau*, *Schielhau*, and *Scheitelhau*, which form the core of Liechtenauer's art. These strikes give a fighter a matrix for judging how to attack an opponent in all positions, and how to defend against their attacks. All positions which can be assumed with any weapon can be placed within the framework of the five strikes. Small differences in the execution of the positions or in the design of the weapons make little or no difference, and require minor adjustments at most.

Such a matrix has two clear disadvantages which Ringeck and Liechtenauer designed the *Zornhau* section to directly addresses. First, this style is quite subtle. It relies on correct execution of the techniques, approaching the opponent in a particular way, and tight control of length and measure. It also requires, and teaches, how to read the opponent. Second, it takes considerable training to learn each component, and then more time to put them together so they can work seamlessly.

The *Zornhau* section, however, offers a complete set of strategies for dealing with an opponent who does virtually anything, and while not always the absolutely optimal move, this section provides a perfect vehicle for training a student to fight, while making sure that they avoid leaving themselves vulnerable to 'advanced techniques.' The *Zornhau* section offers functional, and sometimes optimal, ways to fight just about anyone using just about any weapon. It serves as a primer on the fighting style as a whole, so that a burgeoning young fighter can learn to fight quickly with just a single technique and six fundamental permutations. Indeed, the basic execution of the *Zornhau* can be taught in a few hours, and then used as a framework to teach the broader principles of combat for quite some time before it becomes necessary to add more techniques.

The goal of teaching this section of Ringeck's book should be as much about teaching how to fight in a general sense as it is about teaching how to do the *Zornhau* and its permutations. Concepts like measure, courage, leverage, reading an opponent's intent, feeling the bind, and strategy should, I argue, be considered more important than technical execution, unless the student's lack of proficiency in the given technique prevents them from learning these principles. Stress to your students how the system of strategy makes the individual pieces work together, and how the foundational and advanced techniques fit in so that the students will know how to use what they have learned, and where each will fit in the system once they have completed their training.

The *Zornhau*

Among the ancient masters of the Liechtenauer tradition we find a striking variety of opinions on the *Zornhau*. Ringeck uses the *Zornhau* (the Strike of Wrath) to teach the foundation of this style. The anonymous author of the Codex 44.A.8 which is often, and probably erroneously, attributed to Peter von Danzig, called the *Zornhau* a 'bad peasant blow.'[29] I find this odd considering the amount of space he devotes to it. The logic for this perspective relies on the argument that if one can read the situation well enough, the other four strikes in the system can deal with an opponent in manner superior to the *Zornhau*. Each of the other four strikes breaks a specific guard, and three of them are built with the capacity to strongly counter the most common type of attack, an *Oberhau* (a strike from above) such as the *Zornhau*. One could argue, based on a very limited reading of Danzig, that the best of fencers would never use the *Zornhau* because there is always, theoretically, a better strike to use. This perspective, however, ignores the difference in the ranges that these strikes are used at, and the difficulty of executing the *Zwerchhau*, *Krumphau* and *Schielhau*, all of which require turning the blade onto new angles before the strike can occur, which requires more skill, and often achieving tactical superiority before executing the attack.

Ringeck, on the other hand, holds the *Zornhau* in high esteem, even postulating additional uses for it besides those which appear in other texts of this tradition or the canonical portion of his own text. I have tried to extrapolate his position thus: there is never just one solution to any problem your opponent presents, and the *Zornhau* offers very effective solutions. First, the *Zornhau* will be useful in any situation, as a initial attack, as a follow-up attack, as a *Nachreissen* (pursuing) where you exploit hesitation, or a misjudgment of the measure of the fight by your opponent, or as a defense against quite literally any form of attack. It does not require that you get an exact read on your opponent's actions; a general sense of where the attack comes from will suffice. In three of the four guards this is a known fact, and can be generally deduced from the position of the sword, their feet, and which hand is their sword hand. The *Zornhau* always offers options and, most importantly, is never a mistake to do. The *Zornort*, the defensive version of the technique, can defend against both strikes and thrusts from below as well as those from above, and provides greater options for permutations than any other strike, and a *Zornhau* can easily transition to a *Zornort* as soon as the bind has been made if you end up strong. The Zornhau often will have some advantage in reach, power, leverage, speed, or simplicity compared to other strikes.

Whether as an application for a *Nachreissen*, an opening attack, or a response to a bind where thrusts have failed, the *Zornhau* will threaten your opponent and cover your upper openings well, and it can defend the upper portions of your lower openings if necessary, while your footwork defends your legs. Later in his book, Ringeck even teaches a way of using the *Zornhau* as a solution to the *Zwerchhau*, the blow designed to break not only strikes from above, but the guard (*Vom Tag*) that they are most often thrown from. A cut like the *Zornhau* is also the one prescribed in Leigniczer's sword and buckler section of the Dresden manual, which Ringeck's treatise is also in, for striking an opponent's leg. Dobringer also teaches this variation, and it is quite reasonable to assume that this variation was understood by Ringeck's students.[30]

Second, the *Zornhau* has the greatest combination of speed, reach, cutting power, and options from the bind of any of the five strikes. It is also the hardest strike to simply dodge without engaging the opponent's blade. Indeed, it is, without a doubt, the most physically powerful of the strikes, because it combines the pull of gravity with the turning motion of the body. If you are concerned about penetrating your opponent's clothing, or you want to maximize your chances of inflicting a debilitating injury on your opponent, it is ideal.

Indeed, one could argue the opposite of what von Danzig says. You could learn to fight with just the *Zornhau* against all other strikes and thrusts, and be almost as well off as if you had learned all of the five strikes. In light of this, I argue that the reason the *Zornhau* was taught at all – and I think it important to note that it is taught *first* in the Liechtenauer tradition – was that if someone found themselves in a position where they would need to fight soon, and only had time to learn one strike and its permutations, the *Zornhau* alone could see them through the upcoming conflict if learned correctly. Many sword-fighting styles are built with this kind of strike at their core. The Polish saber styles, for example, were called the 'cross-cutting art,' because of their continuous diagonal strikes which made crosses in the air. Fiore dei Liberi and Philippo Vadi begin nearly all of their plays with the attacker using what they call a *fendente*, a steep diagonal strike which is essentially the same in all important respects as the *Zornhau*.[31]

In short, if you are ever in doubt about what technique to use, use the *Zornhau* or one of its permutations. They are always one of the correct answers to the puzzle your opponent poses. The only limitations are that it cannot be executed from the *Zufechten* directly from the positions *Pflug* (plow) or *Alber* (jester) without first raising the sword and telegraphing your action. This is also true of *Ochs*, but to a lesser extent, requiring only an extended rotation. If you like to start in *Vom Tag* though, then this will not become a problem. The *Zornhau* may have been commonly understood as a beginners' technique by some teachers in this style, it may be inferior to the other five strikes in specific situations, but the *Zornhau* is the closest thing there is to an ultimate technique.

Method: targeting the *Zornhau*

It is very important that you strike the correct target with the correct portion of the blade. From my test cutting experiments, and I have performed and observed more than 1,200 cuts on tatami mats and pork, I have noted that with bastard swords of the types seen in the manuals from this era, you need to strike with the tip at least 4in beyond the target to get good results. The cross-sections of these highly tapered swords cease to be good for cutting around that point. In addition, because the blade needs to be pulled through the target to achieve the appropriate slicing effect, having the blade past the target allows you to draw a great deal more blade through the target, and enhance the cut dramatically. I have also found that this also works well from a tactical perspective because it makes the strike much more difficult for an opponent to simply avoid with footwork. Therefore, I conclude that with bastard swords one should strike so that the weapon extends approximately 4–8in beyond your opponent's body when you begin your attack. You can get closer if you want to, but do not close so much that your opponent can reach out and grab your head or body without stepping. Doing so will permit them to counter virtually any technique with grappling, which makes this a poor choice unless you feel confident that your grappling skills are superior to your opponent's.

A sword with a broad cutting tip, such as a type XIIa or XIIIa, does not need the extra inches to make good cuts, but still benefits from the same tactical and slicing advantages. So even with those I recommend cutting with some of the blade extending past your target at the moment of contact. I should also note that you can cut effectively quite close to the hilt of most European swords, but that they work best when you strike closer to the tip of the blade because that will maximize the speed and the energy of the cut.

Ringeck only says to aim for the head and the body, but we can glean valuable insight by consulting other sources. In spite of his distance from Ringeck in time I find Joachim Meyer's teachings about the *Zornhau* helpful for understanding how to aim it. He says to aim the strike on a downward diagonal line at your opponent's ear, face, or chest. While Meyer uses the forty-five degree angle in his diagram, I have found this problematic in practice. At the forty-five degree angle gravity does not help your cut a great deal, and it becomes easy for a strike made on a steeper angle to become strong in the bind. I think that Meyer's diagram should be taken as a reflection of the Renaissance penchant for making things work with nice even divisions rather than direct advice. The variation in his targeting advice also makes this more likely.[32] Many other manuals with diagrams show much steeper angles for their diagonal cuts. Fiore, for example, whose tradition was contemporary with Liechtenauer's, and used the same type of longsword, aims his *fendente*, an essentially similar strike, from 'teeth to knee', around seventy degrees. I feel that this angle is far more effective in practice, so this is what I teach to my students.[33]

Ringeck has already warned us that if you aim your blade at targets other than your opponent's head or body that your opponent may *Durchwechseln* (change through) and stab you in an exposed opening with little danger to themselves. This happens particularly when one aims too high because with a very small motion the opponent can avoid the strike, and this, I feel, is why Meyer recommends the ear particularly rather than the face. The higher the strike is aimed, the more likely you are to be strong in the bind, but every single student I have taught has

Randy struck his *Zornort* too high. Ben, acting as the teacher, may choose to either demonstrate the result by executing *Durchwechseln*, or he might stop the drill and reset it. This second option is particularly good if Randy already perceived that he made a mistake.

had trouble dealing with the temptation to get 'just a little bit higher'. The theoretical and practical upper limit is a strike between the eyes, but this can be risky because of this temptation. One can know when the opponent is vulnerable to *Durchwechseln* if one can see the underside of their blade at the moment of the bind, or just before. If you can see the underside of your opponent's blade during any long edge *Oberhau* then your opponent's point cannot be threatening you, and you can immediately slip your weapon under theirs, and thrust.

In his manual Ringeck uses *Durchwechseln* as a method to punish poor swordsmanship, and he also explains a special version of it

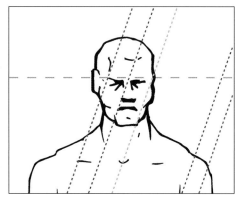

The green line shows Meyer's indicated target, the ear. The blue lines show the upper and lower limits of good targeting for a *Zornhau*, between the eyes and at the chest. The red lines indicate the limits beyond which the strike should be considered botched. If you strike too high your opponent can *Durchwechseln* against you, and if you strike too low you will almost never be strong in the bind.

as a winding to deal with certain complicated binds, rather than as a primary or secondary attack or defense. I believe that Ringeck deliberately left teaching how to execute a *Durchwechseln* for much later in the curriculum. Leaving the bind safely requires some skill to do in practice, and I believe that it should not be frequently attempted by beginners from these initial binds. They are better off practicing correct technique so that they are not open to these kinds of moves. Another reason it may have been left for later is that the thrust from *Durchwechseln* can be difficult to control, and most beginners do not have the control necessary to make it sufficiently accurate or safe with a training partner. Beginning students should, however, be made aware of it so that they understand the consequences of poor execution of their strikes. Advanced students should demonstrate how this happens to newer students as opportunities arise.

Aiming the *Zornhau* too low will leave you open in a different way. If you aim your blow lower than your opponent's shoulder they will likely become strong in the bind, even when your timing was better. This means that they will either hit you with their blow or threaten a direct thrust that will be very hard to counter. The same thing will happen if the blow is done on too shallow an angle. More steeply angled strikes have higher likelihoods of overpowering shallower strikes.

Meyer also mentions that ancient teachers took great pride in striking their opponent and deflecting their blade in the same motion. This indicates that the Liechtenauer tradition's style emphasized attacking with the same motion that they used to defend themselves. It is difficult, but possible to cut an opponent cleanly while in contact with their blade if you are very strong in the bind. The transition to a thrust that Ringeck teaches for the *Zornhau* requires barely any more time, no additional footwork and when done correctly creates the effect Meyer praised, and is much simpler and easier than attempting to do so with a cut.[34]

Tips for teachers: teaching measure

All martial arts teach their students to measure the distance between them and their opponents. Strong grasp of measure allows you to know what you can and cannot do to your opponent from the position you are in, and what they can and cannot do to you in turn. Some styles use a more intuitive method, offering little instruction for concrete application. Some devote a great deal of time and space to it. Ringeck pays scant attention to it, saying only '*Close with your foe so you can cut as you wish, and prevent Durchwechseln from penetrating your shield.*' Remember that the body and sword of a person executing a cut move forward at different rates, and that the final position of a sword whose motion has been arrested by a training partner or weapon may be different from the position it would have been in when contact was made with a cut. Perhaps most importantly, strikes from too far away will miss, and this will open a fighter to *Nachreissen*, which are designed to punish this kind of mistake. Review the explanation of good distance frequently, and make sure your student's drills and sparring show good use of distance consistently.

Each drill I have included here includes an approach phase to make certain that the students will always remember to be training their mastery of measure. Without mastery of this concept no other technique can be learned correctly, because it will be done at the wrong distance. Do not let your students start drills from within distance, or just one step out: this removes the opportunity for crucial training, so they can know when to strike and when they can be struck. Also make sure that the defender does not step into the distance of the attacker if the attacker strikes from out of distance, which will give their training partner a false positive for their judgement of measure.

One particularly subtle point is that because of the order in which Ringeck says you should move your body and weapon, some forward motion of your body and weapon will often occur after you have made contact with your target in a drill. This can be very deceptive in training sessions. I have seen people who do not synchronize their feet or gauge their measure properly have their weapons move as much as 18in forward after their weapon made contact with their opponent's sword or body. Sometimes people will have in fact been striking outside of good cutting range, or hitting only with the very tip of their weapon, but the end position after the motion has stopped will look correct at the end of the action because their body was still moving forward after the motion of the cut had been arrested. Stay aware of this and ensure that you and your students practice striking only at correct measure. It is often helpful to learn measure with a pell so that you can see the effects of your stepping, learn to gauge your range, and refine your footwork.

Remind your students that fighting at proper distance will do ninety percent of the work of keeping their hands and arms safe. The vast majority of the hits that happen to the hands in modern tournaments occur when the fighters are fighting at a distance such that only the hands are in reach. Closing to proper distance as I have described will largely solve this problem.

Remember when approaching an opponent in a sparring match or a real fight that the person to step into the opponent's range will be yielding the *Vor*, and only if the other person hesitates will the person approaching be able to initiate the exchange. Judging from the advice given in this tradition by Ringeck and Dobringer, and my own experience sparring and competing, we see that this frequently happens in sparring, as well as in real fights. This validates that the basic method I've set forth here, with the attacker walking into distance and attacking. I would also suggest that mixing it up, having the defender approach and the attacker beginning their attack when they get into distance, will provide valuable experience as well.

Theory: attacking lower quarters with a *Zornhau*

Against a single weapon there is always one upper quarter open that you can attack, and these quarters are better targets because they are closer and have more vital organs in them. Against two weapons, however, such as the sword and buckler or rapier and dagger, one must often work around the defenses in multiple stages. Often when fighting an opponent with two weapons one must attack the lower quarters. This application of the *Zornhau* isn't covered in Ringeck, but is a reasonable extrapolation from Andre Leigniczer's sword and buckler manual, which is paired with Ringeck's in the Dresden manuscript, and Dobringer's manual, which does mention strikes to the lower quarters.

If you make a *Zornhau* at the lower quarters it should be done as a second or third action. Attacking the lower quarters brings your weapon through *Alber* (the jester's guard), requires a closer than normal distance, and can expose one's

Ben faces Randy with a sword and buckler.

Randy defeats Ben's attack with a *Zornort*, and Ben will wind against it.

Ben winds to thrust at Randy's face. Randy sees this and begins an *Abnemen*, but Ben covers his upper right quarter with his buckler. Randy must now attack a different target.

own upper quarters, so it must be done carefully. With a longsword, if you need to attack the lower quarters, you must create the time and space to do it safely. This can also be viable in longsword vs. longsword fights if, for example, one has come to a relatively close distance in *Ochs*, has one's sword on the outside, and still has the *Vor* while the opponent has closed off the upper openings with a vertical interposition, but these situations arise infrequently.[35]

Randy changes his target, aiming his *Zornhau* at Ben's knee.

Method: learning the *Zornhau*

It is best to learn the cut in the air with a real sword so that you can learn how the real weapon feels, and so you can listen for the whistle that happens when your edge is aligned properly.

We will begin with a cut from right to left. When you execute the Zornhau from the right begin with your left foot forward in the *Vom Tag* position with the sword tucked close to the shoulder with the point extending up and back on roughly a forty-five degree angle. Imagine your opponent coming at you and preparing to do an *Oberhau*. As you imagine them taking that last step which makes them enter good distance begin your *Zornhau*. Make sure when you practice the cut to follow all the way through into *Alber* (the jester's guard).

Place your cut on a roughly seventy-degree diagonal angle set slightly off to the side of your center line so that your blade binds in front of your upper left quarter relative to your opponent. This will create a strong defensive structure which will give you time to react if your opponent becomes strong in the bind. You can achieve this by using your footwork to offset the line you are aiming on vis-à-vis your opponent's body structure, and striking through the center at an angle from a side position relative to your opponent's position. You can also do this by guiding the blade with a bent wrist from a less angular position relative to your opponent. If you are bending your wrist it will be the right wrist when striking from your right while the left wrist remains straight.

Ben stands ready to cut from his right.

Here the arms have left the shoulder, the triceps and pectorals will propel the weapon forward, and begin rotating it.

Here Ben has reached the point of maximum extension for this cut. He will begin pulling the blade backward as it falls toward *Alber*.

Here you can see Ben pulling the sword backward mid-motion.

Your left wrist will bend when striking from the left and the right wrist will remain straight. Always remember to practice appropriate follow through in solo training. Artificially stopping your sword will need to happen to keep your training partner safe in partner drills, and when you practice the *Zornort* by yourself, but you must practice cutting cleanly as well.

When striking from your shoulder your sword arm should begin the blow with a motion very like a straight punch. Remember that your motion must align the edge properly with the plane of the sword's motion. The triceps, pectorals, and shoulder muscles, along with the motion of your torso as it is propelled by your foot

As Ben finishes the cut he turns his hips and torso to settle his weight and lower his center of gravity. This drives the cut downward powerfully and enhances its effect.

and buttocks, must all drive the blow along the desired plane. As your sword moves forward the wrist of your sword arm should extend forward, rotating the blade. At the same time your off-hand should pull the pommel up towards the inside of your sword arm's wrist, snapping the blade forward and giving it extra impetus. Do not bring the pommel all the way to the wrist during the cut: it will weaken the structure of your sword and arms, and decrease the angle of the weapon at the point of contact, decreasing the slicing action of the weapon's motion. The weapon should reach the desired point of maximum extension just as it reaches the target. It should also reach the point where it defends your upper left quarter at that very same moment.

At this point you will begin the follow-through motion. Continue the pull of the triceps, and add some pull from your lats to pull the arms down. Let the blade fall on the angle you have given it until it lands in an *Alber*, or *Pflug* if you are training the *Zornort*. Be sure to pull the weapon back during this motion so that the weapon will slice properly as it goes through the target.

According to Ringeck's teachings your hands and blade should begin the motion. Then begin to step with your right foot using a passing step. After a lot of experimentation I have concluded that your weapon should generally hit before your foot lands. Place your foot so that the toes point toward the opponent. Your back foot should adjust its angle, and/or position, to support your body. With practice this should become one smooth motion.

Where your opponent might potentially move to during your action is irrelevant for the purposes of aiming your strike. You will have to react to it as you feel and see it happen, and not before. You have to threaten them where they are in the moment you choose to strike in order for your attack to work. More importantly, if you are striking at the correct range simply dodging should become nearly impossible.

Method: wrist structure

During a cut the alignment of your edge will chiefly be determined by the way you use your wrist. Ideally, it would always be straight and the whole arm would always be in alignment, and this is taught particularly in single-hand sword styles, but this is not always convenient, possible, or necessary. Simply holding *Vom Tag* above the head will involve bending the wrist. When using a longsword one or the other wrists will frequently need to be bent. However you strike, you must ensure that your technique becomes consistent so that you will perform well under pressure. You must practice it over and over and over again with a real sword, listening for its whistle so that you can do it without thinking. I teach my students that if they are striking from the right, assuming they are right-handed, they can either adjust with footwork and keep their arm straight, or adjust the hands and wrists so that they align the edge with the motion of the blade. Typically I teach that when a student strikes from the right they will bend the right wrist and keep the left arm and wrist straight, lining up the sword with the left arm, and when they strike from the left they hold the entire right arm straight and bend their left wrist.

Drill: targeting the *Zornhau*

Divide the class in two so that everyone faces a training partner. Begin well out of range with enough space so that the students can walk forward and strike with each step so they can perfect their targeting. Have the students take turns being the attacker and advancing striking *Zornhaus* in the air on both sides using their training partner's body to guide

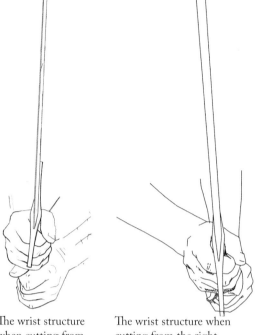

The wrist structure when cutting from the left.

The wrist structure when cutting from the right.

their aiming. After advancing have them strike as they go backwards then have the other member of each partnership do this too. This will allow them to perfect their targeting form on both sides advancing and retreating. Make sure everyone can do it well before moving on. Use this time to correct body mechanics and position.

Drill: *Zornhau* with a moving target

This is a control exercise and teaches you to think clearly when striking and when strikes are coming at you. Provide plenty of space for each pair. If you are in a small room it may be necessary to only have one or two pairs go at a time and have everyone else observe. One partner in the pair will be the defender and the teacher while the other will be the attacker and the student. When the defender calls 'Attack!' the attacker should move to cut when they believe they are in good distance. The defender should move, dodge, and generally make it difficult for the attacker to hit them. If appropriately trained, the defender may also close with their training partner and take a grip of them to stop a blow if the attacker gets too close, but the defender should not make any other offensive actions. This will also help both of them develop strong footwork, and the capacity to read an opponent. Remember correct cutting range places the point of the sword several inches past the target at the point of contact in mid-motion. After twenty or so attempts switch who has the weapon and do the drill again. The goal should be light contact or a clear demonstration that you would have made contact with the correct portion of the blade. When properly trained the attacker should never miss or let the defender close with them unscathed.

Tips for teachers: the *Zornhau*

If you have a trained assistant demonstrate a complete *Zornhau* drill to give your students context for what they are learning. Explain the purpose of each stage of the action and how the fight may be won at each. Make sure as you move on that the students continue to do each individual action correctly and reliably before adding new things to do. When a technique is executed poorly emphasize that the student should not try to force the technique to work or correct it mid-bind after a failed attempt. Instead teach them that a different action would have been called for in the first place, and have them return to their starting positions and try again. For example, if the student is just starting to learn the *Zornort*, and in their attempt to execute it end up weak in the bind, they should stop the drill, back up and try again instead of resisting and trying to work in the bind. That would be appropriate in later drills and sparring matches, but will not help them learn to do the *Zornort* better.

This is also where the student will first be able to internalize the foundations of the style. Make use of every opportunity to bring up the fundamental concepts, especially *Vor*, *Nach*, and *Indes*. Those principles will become the root of the thinking that underlies the strategy we are teaching them to use.

This is also the first opportunity to notice if a person fights timidly. This crucial part of the general teaching is perhaps the most difficult thing to give a student. In ancient times a master might have asked a student to leave the school if they did not make progress on this issue. Our modern context, in which mortal sword combat is almost unheard of, allows us to be more flexible, though in my experience most such persons leave of their own accord soon enough. While I believe that courage can be learned, it cannot really be taught. The student can be guided to it, but it typically comes as a breakthrough, rather than a gradual blossoming as a result of training. If a student proves willing to stick it out, then be patient and supportive and their breakthrough will come.

Lesson 10: The *Zornort*

The Zornhau and its techniques
When a cut comes from above
The Zornort menaces him

Gloss: When someone makes a cut from above at you from their right side you should cut
with a Zornhau, using your long edge, strongly from your right shoulder, and if he is weak
at the sword stab him immediately in the face along his blade. (The Dresden Manuscript)

Method: the *Zornort*

The *Zornort* threatens to end a fight instantly. The blow descends upon the opponent's cut or thrust, landing with the point in front of the opponent's head, and then is instantly thrust forward into the face. An upward thrust through the face threatens brain matter, and the brainstem. Damage here can instantly put an opponent out of commission. The skull has many parts, and is quite hard, so a blade stabbing through it can get stuck relatively easily. When practicing this technique in a drill make sure the withdrawal of the blade is very forceful.

The description and depictions of the *Zornort* (the wrath point), the defensive version of the *Zornhau*, and similar blows from contemporary sources, show the blow being delivered in such a way as to place the point in front of the opponent's face. This can require significant sideways or backwards motion if your opponent is striking so that 4–8in of his blade extends beyond your original position, especially if he has closed the distance so that he's cutting without extending his hands. Be ready to step backward, to either side, or even forward across the line if he attacks from farther away. Over time you will develop a sense of where to step to make your *Zornort* most effective. I recommend using the sideways simple step towards the side the attacking sword is aimed at into a sideways-oriented back-weighted stance, as a good place to start.

Be aware that the distance required to execute the technique correctly is very specific. Too much distance and you will not be able to keep the point threatening the opponent. This will make their counterattack easier, and can even open you up to *Nachresisen* (chasing) or *Durchwechseln* (changing through). Too little distance and your point will be past them and you will have to resort to other techniques such as *Duplieren* (doubling), *Winden* (winding), *Mutieren* (transforming), *Zucken* (yanking/beating), or *Ringen* (grappling).

Because of this, executing this interpretation of the defensive *Zornort* is usually best done with a closer cutting technique with a motion like that shown in Paulus

Kal to bring your strong onto their weak. This helps maintain leverage on your opponent's blade, and keeps you close enough so that you can thrust a considerable distance from the position your blade achieves. Teach your students that they control the distance with their footwork, and their hands. Be aware that if you do not extend enough you can actually make yourself weak in the bind if you do not adjust to the angle of your opponent's cut, and that the same can happen if you extend too much at the wrong distance. Perhaps most importantly, if you pre-empt the attack you will end up beneath the opponent's weapon and become weak in the bind, unable to make the following thrust.

Begin out of distance. Randy, the attacker, calls 'Draw!' and Ben, the defender, calls 'Attack!'

Randy moves in and attacks.

Ben strikes his *Zornort*, landing atop the middle of Randy's sword, and thrusts the point toward Randy's face. As he does so Ben steps to his left with a sideways simple step to gain more leverage in the bind, and he lets his right foot follow to create a stable position.

Drill: the *Zornort*

Now we designate one person as the attacker and teacher, and one person as the defender and student. Begin from well out of distance. The attacker approaches and does a *Zornhau*. The defender will cut a *Zornhau* too so that they land on top of the opponent's blade with their point in front of the attacker's face. This will create a bind, and the defender should have a distinct leverage advantage from being on top and having their hands closer to the bind than their opponent. When done well the defender's point will land in front of the attacker's face.

Begin well out of distance so that you always practice gauging length and measure.

Ben enters correct distance and attacks. When doing this drill use as much force and intent as you safely can. Be sure that you deliver the blow with the correct portion of the blade, and strong footwork.

Randy responds by taking a small passing step back with his left foot and binds on top of Ben's blade, becoming strong in the bind and threatening a thrust to the face.

Tips for teachers: common pitfalls in learning the *Zornort*

Many students I teach have difficulty overcoming the fear of their opponent's weapon. This can lead to falling into two very bad habits: not committing to their strikes when they attack, and aiming at their opponent's sword instead of their opponent when they defend.

Against unskilled fighters who do not know how to exploit these problems it can feel good to do this because you can guarantee you will be strong in the bind, or at least strong enough to not get hit in the initial attack. The problem with this result is that you will not threaten your opponent when you do this, and therefore gain no advantage when making this defense. Worse, both of these habits can be easily exploited by a skilled fighter, and could get you instantly killed. These problems can also be quite hard to detect for the students. They will often only realize what they are doing if you tell them and show them over and over again.

When someone attacks with their *Zornhau*, and does not commit to their attack, letting their fear of their opponent dominate their action, they anticipate the counterattack, and withhold their sword at a raised partially extended position instead of committing all the way into the strike at their opponent's body. They will often leave their hands up high, or even reverse the motion and lift their hands after the bind, sometimes without fully extending the blade much at all. This drastically changes the way a drill plays out. It becomes impossible to hit with a *Zornort* if the attacker's *Zornhau* is done this way. Students who do this will often end the drill with their hands at the height of their face, or well off to the side after contact. When done correctly their blade should be in front of their shoulders, heart, or belly as shown in the original *fechtbucher*. These elevated or offset positions, combined with the high hands, prevent the first techniques of this section from succeeding. Doing so, however, fails to gain the *Vor*, and it leaves you open to *Durchwechseln* (changing through), and *Abnemen* (upwards disengagement).

When someone is defending with their *Zornort* and fights the sword, on the other hand, they will become strong in the bind, and prevent the initial blow from hitting them, but they will also fail to hit their opponent, or gain the *Vor*. If the attacker seizes the initiative with a *Durchwechseln* or any following cut, what Dobringer called the *Nachschlag*, they will keep the *Vor*. Both of these mistakes make a defense, but yield the *Vor* to the opponent, and the follow-up techniques available to the opponent will likely win the fight.

You can help a student overcome this by training with them in a way that puts them under considerable pressure and forewarning them that when they make these mistakes you will use the appropriate counter-technique to illustrate what the error would leave them open to. You should also have them practice striking with intent

Randy has struck too high in an effort to become strong in the bind. He has become strong in the bind, but his weapon is much too high to threaten his opponent. Because of this Ben can respond with *Durchwechseln*.

and control in low-pressure contexts so that they can focus on form. Emphasize that Ringeck's first techniques are designed for fighting skilled fighters, that good fighters in this style either commit to their strikes, or they do not make them at all, and they always fight the opponent, not their weapon. The only way to break the instinct is to have them train extensively, coaching them to have the right mindset, and showing them how their errors would be punished by a skilled opponent until they develop new instincts. If you make sure they understand just how devastating these mistakes can be, you will inspire them to work hard and improve.

Make sure you have your students push their levels of speed, intent, force and control to get the most realistic results possible. Never let them become complacent in drills like this.

Theory: the *Zornort* with Goliath footwork

In the Goliath manual we see the person thrusting from the bind having stepped in front of his left foot with his right foot. This can be advantageous because it moves our strong toward our opponent's weak, especially if they start their attack from very far away, and it can certainly throw your opponent off if they are unaccustomed to the angles it creates. We see many steps across the line like this in the Glasgow version of Ringeck, but, unfortunately, none of the art is given for the *Zornhau*. We can easily extrapolate that it is likely that Ringeck taught this version of the technique as it is extant in a later manual within the tradition, and the footwork exists in his own book. It is a less natural position, and takes some practice to do well. You may wish to leave variations like this till the end of the *Zornhau* curriculum.

Here we stand in a facsimile of the image of the *Zornort* in the Goliath *fechtbuch*. Randy has approached and struck from his right. Ben has struck a *Zornort* by stepping to the left across the line with his right foot aiming his foot at Randy. The image in the manual shows the figure on the left's arms being quite extended, as if maximum extension was achieved from just out of distance, which may have been for safety, or demonstration purposes, but this is a convention common in the medieval and Renaissance *fechtbucher* tradition. The high hands represent the end of an extended thrust, not the point of the initial bind. The manual also shows the figure on the right leaning back, as if flinching from the blow, or making space for the technique to work safely in practice.

Here you can see the Goliath *Zornort* with the thrust finished in the air at the point of maximum extension.

Here you can see the footwork of the Goliath *Zornort* from the front.

When executing the *Zornort* by this method you step across the line with your right foot, angling it toward your opponent, and angling your back foot outward to create a large trapezoid with the balls and heels of your feet for your center of gravity to sit in. This should move you a great distance towards the weak of your opponent's sword. The stance at the end of the strike requires practice to do in a stable fashion. Be sure that the ball of your foot lands first, and that the foot presses down and outward from the ball and the heel, and that the rear foot also presses in the opposite direction with both the ball and heel. This will greatly improve the stability of your final position.

This technique requires a larger than normal distance, because if your opponent can close the distance to grapple your stance will be ill suited to oppose it. Make sure that your opponent is well out of grappling distance if you wish to use this version of the technique. As such this technique is best done if the opponent initiated their attack from very far away. Once the bind has been made and you have established that you are strong extend your sword forward toward the face. You may extend your hands and weapon as shown in the facsimile here so you can cross the entire distance efficiently. Your follow-up step for the following cuts should be done by stepping out in the same direction that the first foot went in. So if you began with a passing step across the line with your right foot to your left and your opponent winds, and you need to attack his other opening with a cut, then you will do so with a passing step to the left continuing in the same direction that you began with around your opponent.

Lesson 11: *Abnemen*

Another technique of the Zornhau
If he perceives your attack, disengage upwards, and drive on.

Gloss: When you thrust against his face from the Zornhau, if he senses it and parries with the strong of his sword, then swiftly wrench your sword up around his, and strike at his head from the other side across the angle made by his blade. (The Dresden Manuscript)

Theory: the *Abnemen*

Later on, after the section on winding where the counter to this technique is taught, this move is named '*Abnemen.*' Tobler translated it literally as 'take away,' and I translate it as 'disengage,' 'disengagement,' or 'upwards disengagement.' If you wish to use the German call it '*Abnemen,*' and if you wish to use English call it a 'disengagement' or an 'upwards disengagement.'

The crux of interpreting this technique lies in what is meant by '*versetzt den Stich mitt Storcke*' which is the description of the opponent's defense that the 'disengage upwards' is done to counter. Tobler and Forgeng both interpret it literally as 'parries with strength', which they take to understand as using muscle, rather than leverage, to directly oppose the thrust. They both take this to mean a lateral motion which does not threaten the opponent. I have two strong objections to this interpretation. First, that sort of defense is the precise sort of thing that Ringeck warns not to do early in the manual, and he has already stated that when someone does this you can change through (*Durchwechseln*) against him, which would be a preferred response to this kind of mistake. If someone made such a mistake then the only situation in which one should beat the blade and cut instead of *Durchwechseln* (changing through) would be if your opponent happened to be at a distance too close to thrust, but too far away to grapple, in which case the action interpreted by Forgeng for '*ruck dein Schwert ubersich oben ab von dem sinen und haw im zu der anderen Sytten*' by violently lifting the sword directly up to beat the weapon with the cross, and disengaging to cut to the other side, would work fine, but only at that very specific distance. That action can be very effective, and I interpret that action as the most likely interpretation of the *Zucken* in the advanced techniques sections, which I hope to be able to address in the future, but that lies beyond the scope of this book. I believe it was taught in that place, rather than here, because it requires superior grasp of measure to be able to execute well, and few people at this early stage of training possess the capacity for controlling and reading measure well enough to know the difference. If you are too close you will expose yourself to grappling or hand slices, and if you are too far away you will expose your hands to *Durchwechseln*.

My second objection is that if we have the opponent do Tobler and Forgeng's interpretation we must embrace a teaching pedagogy that disconnects the techniques of this section from Ringeck's warning and admonition that it should be countered with *Durchwechseln*, and, perhaps more importantly, doing so fails to connect this technique to the other techniques ordered around it. I propose instead that the language of this section derives

Randy senses the threat from Ben winding his sword at his face and wrenches his sword upward so that his blade slopes down and forward to his right. From here he will cut a *Zornhau* at Ben's right ear.

from the same verbiage used by Liechtenauer in the following section on winding, which I translate as 'become stronger as you resist him and thrust.' Ringeck there describes a winding with a rolling action as you move the sword to an *Ochs* position and thrust forward at the face. This interpretation allows the techniques to feedback one into another with the students learning two sides of the same sequence for these initial sections. It also avoids having them practice techniques which were warned against by Ringeck, and potentially developing bad habits. For these reasons I interpret '*versetzt den Stich mitt Storcke*' as 'parries with the strong of his sword.' I interpret this as the winding of the following section. For the above reasons I believe these first two sections simply provide the offensive and defensive sides of a single introductory sequence used for teaching new students the most important lessons of sword play.

At this point Ringeck is still dealing with the defensive side of this technique, and he will complete his explanation of this before moving on to the offensive side. Having struck the *Zornort* from the right, as soon as you feel that your point is going to fail to hit your target rotate your weapon so that your hilt is up above your upper left quarter and your point is angled down on an angle that descends from just above your eyes past a point just above your shoulder and further down and forward to your right. This creates a barrier between you and your opponent's weapon that cannot be safely circumvented by *Durchwechseln*, or overpowered with strength. From here step forward, and to the left, with a passing step to ensure that your opponent's point does not threaten you. The natural rotation of your body will help with this. Once you are clear of the point strike at his head from the other side with another *Zornhau*. Should the opponent attempt to wind against it to *Ochs* on their other side as well, your blade should land on their blade and you should be able to attempt the technique again on the other side.

Method: the *Abnemen*

The *Abnemen* works much like a classic Moulinet, but the physical mechanics are a little different because of the nature of the two-handed weapon. To do the *Abnemen* lift your hilt and blade until the entire plane made by your sword is above your head. You should be able to see your opponent beneath your blade. Keep the point forward toward your opponent, but not aimed directly at them, to prevent the possibility of *Durchwechseln*. Once you have accomplished this, begin to move forward and to the side, past your opponent's point, with a passing step, and cut at their head with another *Zornhau* from the other side.

Randy has wound threatening Ben's face.

Ben Begins the *Abnemen*, raising his sword to defeat the thrust. He will now move forward and cut at Randy's head.

Drill: the *Abnemen*

Execute this exactly as the *Zornort* drill, striking from the right as before, but this time we will add another move. The attacker will be the teacher and the defender will be the student. When the defender calls 'Attack!' the attacker will approach and strike a *Zornhau* at good distance. The defender will execute a *Zornort*. When he

Ben has approached and attacked. As he does so Randy strikes down with his own *Zornhau* hoping to place his point in front of Ben's face and stab. At this moment Ben senses that he is weak in the bind and will begin his winding.

Ben senses he is weak in the bind and begins to wind towards Randy's face. Randy, sensing the threat Ben is posing, must begin his defense.

Randy wrenches his blade upward deflecting Ben's point. He then steps past the point of Ben's sword. He now has a clear opening to strike at Ben's right side.

Randy completes his cut, striking with a *Zornhau* just below Ben's Ear. He lets his right foot follow his motion to stabilize his stance in the new position.

feels his point being displaced the attacker will begin to wind against it. When the defender feels his thrust beginning to be displaced they will execute the Abnemen (disengage upwards) by rotating their sword up so that their hilt and blade are above their eyes to protect the upper quarter. As they do this, they will let their point hang down and forward to their right to keep their opponent's point from threatening them. The strong of their sword and their cross must be angled to guard their hands against an upwards motion of the attacker's sword. Once they have removed the threat, they should begin a passing step forward and to their left, landing on the ball of their foot, and as the foot settles down aiming it toward their opponent. This often involves a certain amount of pigeon-toeing, so that their body can rotate using it as a stable support structure, which will frequently require an adjustment or stabilizing step of their other foot. As the defender's body clears the point they must begin rotating their torso and bringing their sword up and around so that they can strike on a steep diagonal with another *Zornhau* from the other side.

Tips for teachers: *Abnemen*

Recite the original teachings for the *Abnemen* to your students. This technique requires three correctly done actions to happen before it can be properly executed: the *Zornhau*, the *Zornort*, and the *Winding*. Always ensure that every action up to the one the drill is designed to emphasize is done correctly. Stop and reset when a blow is cleanly struck or demonstrated, even if they do not get to the *Abnemen*. Also do this if a different mistake is made. There is no point in teaching a move against a situation it was not designed to deal with until the student has a firm grasp of the foundation of their chosen style.

    After they become skilled enough to reliably execute these moves in their ideal forms begin having them execute each technique as they feel their opponent's defense begin, rather than after each action is completed. Be sure to use proper striking technique on the second and third cuts. This often becomes sloppy under pressure, so watch for it.

Lesson 12: *Winden*

Another technique of the Zornhau

Become stronger as you resist him
Thrust, if he notices it, then take him low

Gloss: When you strike a Zornhau, *and he parries it, becoming strong on the sword, hold strongly against it yourself. With the strong of your sword move up to the weak of his blade. As you do this, wind your hilt in front of your head, while remaining on the sword, thrusting into his face from above.* (The Dresden Manuscript)

Theory: the *Winding*

Winding glues the entire corpus of the tradition together and the capstone technique of the style is 'The Eight Windings,' an extrapolation and elaboration on this fundamental technique in all the ways it can be applied. It serves as the quickest defense to being weak in the bind, and offers an immediate, and deadly counter-attack in the same motion. A small variation on this technique, the *Mutieren*, gives us a response to an opponent's winding as is depicted in the Codex Wallerstein and Paulus Kal. We will address this in detail later in this volume.[36]

I interpret and teach this technique as the attacker's reaction to the *Zornort*. Liechtenauer's *Merkverse* describes this technique in the original German thusly: '*versetzt den Stich mitt Storcke.*' I translate this as 'parry the thrust with the strong.' Ringeck's gloss of this section describes it as an action where we turn the long edge toward the opponent's weapon, and, as we make this rolling action, we raise the sword so that we aim our own thrust at our opponent's face with the same action.

Note that you cannot do this technique effectively if the opponent does a lateral parry, aiming the sword away from you, instead of a *Zornort*. Ringeck, however, views this as a classic mistake in his fighting theory because it leaves one open to *Durchwechseln* and *Abnemen*.

Method: *Winding*

If you feel that your opponent has become strong in the bind, and that they are threatening you with their point then roll your sword so that the long edge points up and out on a diagonal angle, push your hilt up to *Ochs* so that you can look under your sword near the side of your head, ideally just above your eyes, to protect your upper quarter. The point should hang down just slightly towards your opponent's face. As you do this push the sword forward to thrust through the face. Depending on the distance between you and your opponent, if you draw the blade back as you wind up to *Ochs* you extend the distance between your point and your opponent's face, increasing the time your opponent has to react. So make certain that you are pressing forward toward the opponent's face as you wind the weapon and aim your thrust. The point should end just in front of your training partner's face when training without protective gear. When training solo, and with masks practice full extension.

Tips for teachers: pitfalls in teaching *Winding*

The defender must be strong in the bind, and attempting to threaten you with their point, for *Winding* to work as described. Unless the attacker can execute their *Zornhau* well, and the defender can execute their *Zornort* well, learning *Winding* will not work. Both participants must commit deep into the techniques and not raise their hands to try to become artificially strong in the bind and block the attack, which would leave them open to *Durchwechseln*, or at closer distances *Abnemen*. The students at the stage I am speaking of here are just beginning their training to feel the bind. Most of them will have an instinct to lift their arms to block the incoming thrust, or push it sideways with an upturned point when they become weak in the bind. As teachers of this style, we need to break this instinct.

You will know when they make this mistake because they will become strong in the bind, but they will achieve a position that fails to threaten their opponent with their point. Teach them that this action might prevent the thrust, but it fails to seize the *Vor*. If they do this their teacher should *Durchwechseln* (change through), or use *Abnemen*, or, if the situation calls for it, *Zucken*, *Hend Drucken* (press/slice the hands), or *Durchlauffen* (running through/grappling) also offer options to a person who still has the *Vor* after their attack.

Drill: *Winding*

The attacker will be the student and the defender the teacher. The attacker approaches and cuts a *Zornhau*. The defender cuts a *Zornort*. The attacker then rolls their sword's long edge towards their opponent's weapon and lifts their arms, moving their blade up so that it is roughly parallel with the ground, or angled slightly downwards, at the height of their face, aiming the point of their sword so they can stab them in the face.

Ben takes the role of the attacker and Randy will be the defender. Ben approaches and attacks with a *Zornhau*.

Randy responds with a small passing step back, and strikes with a *Zornort*. Ben feels that he has become weak in the bind, and will start the *Winden*.

Tips for teachers: 'beginning to feel'

Unless you are training with someone who is very skilled and is deliberately trying to give only a certain kind of bind there is no guarantee in the first few months of training as to whether one student will be weak or strong at the sword. If new students must practice together then, unfortunately, we modern practitioners must practice the phases of the technique in a slightly different order than they are presented in Ringeck's manual. The following drill is designed to help students learn this core principle.

Ben begins his *Winding* by rolling the sword's long edge towards Randy's blade, angling it up and out on a diagonal angle. In this position Ben will need to pull his point back just a tiny bit so that he can thrust, but this will not always be necessary. Emphasize that in a real fight the thrust can begin before the winding has even been completed. The *Winding* should, ideally, attack as well as defend.

Ben finishes his winding locking Randy's blade between the strong of his sword and his cross. Ben's sword is aimed squarely at Randy's face with a very slight downward angle. In a real fight, or a sparring match with helmets, Ben would thrust forward to complete the technique.

Drill: feeling the bind

This drill requires that all participants have established a strong level of control. The teacher will be the attacker and the student the defender. The student will call for the attack and will simply make *Zornhau* with force and intent, landing it with control in the correct position, and do nothing else. The student will attempt a *Zornort*, and feel the bind in an attempt to discern whether they are weak or strong, and thrust with a *Zornort* or use *Winden* appropriately. Reset after the first reaction to the bind. Ideally the student should have scored a clear hit either with a *Zornort* or a Winding. The teacher must note if the student made the wrong choice. Be aware, that if a *Zornort* is executed when the student is weak it will not hit, but if the *Winden* is used when the student is strong, they will hit, but have wasted time. Make sure you point out particularly the second situation.

It is of utmost importance that the blows be thrown at proper range and at correct targets. This is the number one thing the teacher should be trying to watch for at this stage. Many people do not get close enough to hit their opponent's head or body with their initial offensive strikes. You should not move on to this stage of training unless the previous material can be done reliably. If students begin making lots of mistakes in this drill, have them step back and relearn the previous material.

The students may be overcompensating, over-anticipating the strike, flinching and lifting their sword in response to the bind, or they may be striking too high or out of range. Emphasize that they should perform no follow-up maneuvers whatsoever from the initial bind and thrusts.

The teacher in the drill should strive to make their strikes with force, and intent. The student should feel under significant pressure to do their technique correctly.

Have participants trade roles after ten repetitions. Then practice it again, striking from the opposite side. Then change partners and do it again. Instruct the group that if someone strikes out of range, or strikes too high, their partner should notify them. If necessary, work with the student yourself and demonstrate the consequences of leaving yourself open to *Durchwechseln* 'changing through' or *Nachreissen* 'chasing.' Advanced students should forewarn their partners, and simply execute these techniques when the opportunity arises to show their partner what would happen if they make these mistakes.

Ben approaches and attacks. Randy, playing the role of the teacher, will simply present the bind. Ben, playing the role of student, will feel the bind to learn whether he is weak or strong, and respond either by thrusting with the *Zornort*, or *Winding*.

Here Ben senses that he has become strong in the bind and will thrust to the face.

Here Ben senses that he has become weak in the bind and will wind.

Lesson 13: Thrust over the *Abnemen*

Another technique of the Zornhau

If you thrust high from the Winding, as described, and he parries the thrust by raising his arms and his hilt, then stay in the Winding, move the point down, between his arms, and thrust to his breast. (The Dresden Manuscript)

Theory: '*setz im den ort niden zwischen sinen armen un der brust*'

This portion of text from Ringeck explains the last line of the *merkverse* mentioned in Lesson 12, where the *Winding* is introduced 'if he sees it, then take him low'. Based on the description Ringeck offers, I agree with Lindholm's interpretation. The defender begins to use *Abnemen* after the *Winden*, the attacker simply reaches higher up so that they can thrust over the *Abnemen*, before it can disengage from the bind, and they plant their thrust into the breast between the defender's arms.

I would like to note a particular difference here between Ringeck and Paulus Kal. In Paulus Kal's *Fechtbuch* we see a different application of the same lines of Liechtenauer's *merkverse*, which we will deal with in later lessons. Kal's text is quite terse, and I translate the relevant line as a variation of the Recital's line 'If he notices it, then take him low.' The technique which he shows differs greatly from Ringeck's gloss at this point: it seems to skip this technique entirely. I, therefore, conclude that Kal is in fact showing a different technique altogether, referring to the application of his recommended movement in *Krieg*, rather than a permutation of the initial *Winden*, per se.

In Kal's *Fechtbuch* the technique shown seems to be a Durchwechseln to a lower opening, there is no targeting of a thrust between the arms to the breast, either underneath or over. The arms of the opponent are not raised, and the thrust is aimed towards the belly, not the breast. In short, it doesn't match Ringeck's description at all. In Kal's depiction the attacker seems to have left the bind after a bad parry, and thrusts to the first convenient lower opening with their Durchwechseln.[37]

This image in Kal surprised me a great deal. In order to do this technique safely within the fencing theory of Ringeck, the opponent must make a mistake, what Ringeck would assess to be an ineffective defense that fails to threaten the opponent. It also requires that the student learn to read this kind of mistake very early on. They must be able to tell when they have an opening big enough to do the technique, and when they do not. The teacher who trains the student needs enough experience to not develop bad habits when they make this mistake, and this makes it inappropriate if your group does not have a large number of experienced teachers, or advanced students, who can initiate the newer students into this.

I've tried to reconcile these sources, to see if there is some way these two masters could possibly be doing the same technique, but the only thing they have in common is Liechtenauer's *merkverse* which says 'If he sees it strike low', which Ringeck disconnects as part of a previous paragraph. I believe we should take the evidence from these sources at face value, and conclude that even though they came from the same tradition, that they are actually teaching something quite different from each other at this point. If we interpret these first techniques in Ringeck as connected, flowing into and out of each other, elegantly giving us a single set of exercises to not only teach someone superior fighting techniques, but also a way to learn the general principles of fighting, and how to develop the core of your offense and defense, and if we allow that Ringeck largely leaves teaching the execution of *Durchwechseln* to later in his manual, which he plainly does, then this conclusion makes sense, and it is how I choose to interpret this section of Ringeck's book.

Here we see Kal's interpretation of 'if he sees it strike low.' Randy made a bad parry against Ben's sword pushing it laterally to his left without threatening Ben, so Ben executes a *Durchwechseln* to the lower openings.

Now I wish to clarify that I do not think that Kal's technique is poor technique. In fact, if your opponent does what he depicts, then it is an excellent application of *Durchwechseln*. I simply do not think that it matches the technique that Ringeck describes. I do not feel surprised that we find some differences like this between these masters, even important differences, which demand strong pedagogical changes. Such things are normal in the modern world, even between teachers of the same tradition. Trying to reconcile different masters of this tradition has some merit if we are trying to divine what Liechtenauer taught, however, we must allow that differences of understanding, preference, methodology, pedagogy, style, and interpretation of Liechtenauer's original teachings, may be incompatible between masters within this tradition. This is the chief reason that I focus on studying and practicing Ringeck, rather than trying to reconstruct original Liechtenauer, or a synthesis of his tradition.

I argue that there is no reason to believe that Liechtenauer's original teaching was necessarily superior to the teachings of his students or their students after them until the mid-1500s when the role of the longsword in self-defense, duels of honor, and warfare, began to change. If differences exist not only between his followers, but also between Liechtenauer and those who came after them in his tradition, then we must acknowledge the possibility that his students may have made improvements on his original work, or they may have let it degrade, or simply have embraced stylistic differences without it affecting the overall quality. The end of Ringeck's manual, for example, includes material supplementary to Liechtenauer's original *Merkverse* which he felt compatible with the style and worth teaching. It is also simply possible that Liechtenauer's teaching here was more general and that he expected his students to differ in their applications of his teachings. This seems consistent with works by authors such as Jorg Willhalm Hutter, for example.[38]

Method: Ringeck's between the arms and thrust to his breast

As your opponent begins their *Abnemen* you will forestall the attack by lifting your hilt and attempting to get behind their sword with your point. Reach over their blade, thrusting down towards the breast as they begin to withdraw their point from the bind. I find that this is far more likely to hit than aiming for the face because it makes contact farther down toward the weak of their blade, and has greater leverage. In practice this is a slightly more risky technique than we usually find in this style, in that if you fail to hit with it you have used up time which you will need to make the follow-up defense. This of course must be weighed against the fact that swordplay is risky, period, and that the same could be said of any move. It's just even more true here.

Drill: between the arms and thrust to his breast

The attacker approaches and does the *Zornhau*. The defender executes a *Zornort*. The attacker winds against it. The defender attempts *Abnemen*. The attacker attempts to raise their sword and thrust over the *Abnemen* at the breast between the arms. Let the natural course of events happen. Whichever of the students does their technique most swiftly and correctly should be able to demonstrate a hit. As this thrust does not threaten the face contact is allowable.

After the initial exchange Randy senses that his thrust has been displaced and he attempts to use *Abnemen* so he can strike a *Zornhau* to the other side. Ben feels his action in the bind and will respond with a thrust between Randy's arms towards the breast.

Here Ben executes the thrust by reaching up over Randy's sword and thrusting downwards into Randy's chest.

Lesson 14: Breaking the *Abnemen*

Breaking the Abnemen
Note: When you bind at the sword with strength and your adversary pulls his sword upwards and strikes at your head from the other side, bind strongly with the long edge and attack his head from above. (The Dresden Manuscript)

Theory: interpreting clues from the *Winden* and *Abnemen*

In this section we find the term that gives a name to the 'disengage upwards' described as a counter to the winding in the previous sections, '*Abnemen*'. The technique also receives its clearest description here, wrenching the sword upward and striking at the head from the other side.

Method: breaking the *Abnemen*

If your opponent manages to successfully begin a second strike to your other opening, you will defend with another *Winden*. Simply take a passing step back or out to the side, wind your sword in front of your head, and end in an *Ochs* position on the right side, with the cross just in front of your face, and the hilt just above your eyes. Make sure that the cross of your weapon is aimed diagonally up and outward on an angle a little shallower than his cut, so that the cross can catch his blade and protect your hands and face. Aim the long edge at his blade, bind against his weapon with the strong of your sword, and hit him in the face with a thrust. This should be one simple clean motion. These last two actions, the *Abnemen* and the Breaking the *Abnemen*, can be repeated over and over again, as counters to the other person's move.

Drill: breaking *Abnemen*

As always begin from well out of distance. The attacker approaches, and executes the *Zornhau*. The defender executes a *Zornort*. The attacker winds against it. The defender uses *Abnemen* to cut at the other side. The attacker winds their sword to the other side to meet the new *Zornhau*

Ben has wound against Randy's *Zornort*.

Randy senses Ben has become strong in the bind and begins his *Abnemen*.

Ben senses Randy become strong in the bind and is beginning the *Abnemen*. He passes backwards and wind his sword in front of his face to cover his upper right quarter.

As Randy completes his second *Zornhau* Ben intercepts it, catching Randy's sword on his strong and cross, and thrusts to the face.

Randy begins his *Abnemen* on the other side so he can strike at Ben's upper left quarter.

Ben begins a passing step backwards and winds to cover his upper left quarter.

Here we see the third *Winden* finished and Ben thrusting towards Randy's face from a compact back-weighted stance where he will complete his thrust at Randy's face.

with a step back or out. They should position themselves so that they can thrust from the new bind to the head.

After the students become used to this, add one or more repetitions of the *Abnemen* and a final *Winden*. You may even permit them to do this until one or the other of them clearly demonstrates a hit, or, if wearing masks, is struck. While the demonstration shows ideal completed positions, the actions will only be completed when fighting in earnest if they succeed. Some half-finished technique, may therefore, be symptomatic of good fencing, as long as each technique shows clear execution and intention.

Tips for teachers: *Abnemen*

While your edge should hit your opponent's flat, some edge-on-edge contact can happen, but the oblique angle of this should ensure that it is not likely to damage real swords. Ensure that the students use *Winden* to aim a thrust and do more than simply block, and be sure they don't beat the blade off to the side with this action. At this point the student has a single complete technique and set of responses. They should begin to train while actively resisting each other's techniques and respond dynamically to them. This drill should become sparring with a complete, if limited, technique set. Remember as the intensity of the training increases there is a significant temptation to attempt a technique beyond the limits of your control. Constantly remind people to maintain a safe level of control. Watch your students carefully to make sure they do not hurt each other and that they internalize their commitment to their training partner's safety.

Theory: reverse grip *Winding*

After examining the images of using reverse grips in other techniques of the Glasgow version of Ringeck, the Goliath *fechtbuch*, Fiore's *Fior di Battaglia*, Jorg Wilhelm Hutter's *fechtbuch*, and Hans Talhoffer's *fechtbuch*, I concluded that the reverse grip was a practical variation on winding actions used by a number of teachers of different styles, including Ringeck, and in this technique specifically. I felt it would be worth including this variation to show the breadth of possibility in the execution

Ben has wound and Randy begins his *Abnemen*.

Here Ben begins a reverse grip winding with a passing step back and to his right. His right arm begins moving to his right, remaining in the same wound position, while the left hand turns to the other side of the pommel so it can exert leverage in the same direction.

Here Ben finishes this winding, using the leverage of his left arm to set his sword in front of his upper right quarter so he can thrust to at Randy. If Randy executes another *Abnemen* he can wrench the blade in front of his upper left quarter quite easily while maintaining distance with his footwork.

of the technique. I will use Ringeck's particular version of the reverse grip for the instruction and images below.

This version of the *Winden* is slightly faster than regular winding action, and requires less footwork than regular winding. It has, however, less reach in the thrust, and a more restricted range of motion in general. It also is a little more complicated to cut from than a normal grip. Should you need to cut, you will need to change your grip back to the normal grip before you can execute it properly.

To perform the grip change, release the fingers of the off-hand from the pommel, but maintain contact with your palm on the pommel. Turn the off-hand to the other side of the handle, and grip the handle with a reverse grip from the other side. This provides a very strong structure to make swift windings, with a lot of leverage to resist the opponent.

Lesson 15: *Krieg*

Attend to another good lesson

Pay close attention
Cut, Thrust, Guard, Weak or Strong
Indes, and drive Nach
Enter Krieg carefully, and without haste
He who follows Krieg above
Will find shame below.

Gloss: If they bind at your sword with a strike or a thrust, you must immediately perceive if they are weak or strong at the sword. When you sense this, you shall know in that very moment if it is better to fight him in the Vor, or the Nach. You shall not rush to use Krieg, for Krieg is nothing other than Winden at the sword.

In Krieg you should do this: When you cut at him with a Zornhau and he parries it, raise your arms and wind the point to the upper opening. When he parries the thrust, stay in the winding and thrust to the lower opening. If he follows your sword to parry it, then lead your point through under his, hang your point from above, to the other side, and thrust to the other opening on his right side. This is how you can defeat him above and below with Krieg. (The Dresden Manuscript)

Theory: *Indes, Vor* and *Nach*

The first paragraph introduces '*Indes.*' Others, translate 'indes' as 'simultaneously,' or 'immediately,' but I prefer to translate it as 'in the moment' or 'at the moment'. Therefore, we should know 'at the very moment' our weapon meets the opponent's weapon which techniques we will next use, by sensing his pressure and leverage through our hands. The process must become instinctive. Quality and speed of judgement *Indes* can only be acquired through experience with active binding and winding against a non-compliant opponent, usually in sparring or very carefully structured drills. If we are bound, but strong we should feel that we have the *Vor*. In the bind weak and strong correspond first and foremost to the possibility of executing a clean thrust with minimal changing of the position, and this corresponds with *Vor* and *Nach*. If we feel we are weak in the bind, we must recognize that we are in the *Nach*. We must deal with our opponent's threat before we may attack safely. Our goal is to take the *Vor* away from our opponent so that they must respond to us.

Theory: the role and execution of Krieg

Other fighting styles often treat extended working in the bind as anathema. Most swordsmen I've seen naturally favor a strategy like that described by George Silver, who teaches that you should enter, strike, and then quickly leave distance and spend most of the fight out of distance unless you intend to grapple with your opponent up close. Liechtenauer and Ringeck present a much more aggressive strategy, and merely advise caution. For this fighting style the chief question is how ready the opponent is for this kind of offense. Once a fighter in this style commences combat they feel in the bind, relying on their sense of touch to give them the data they need to take their opponent apart. They never give their opponent any breathing room. As soon as they sense an attack they defend in a way that threatens the opponent at the same time. They attack as soon as they see which opening they can attack safely. When they sense a defense they feel to detect if there is an actual threat from it. If there is no threat they proceed to attack the next opening. If there is a threat they neutralize it and immediately attack the next opening, ideally with the same motion.

The second paragraph in Ringeck's section on *Krieg* describes a series of *Winding* and *Durchwechseln*. There are multiple techniques which might fit the description of the text, and I believe this ambiguity may very well be intentional. Liechtenauer's description seems to inextricably connect with the following section, which instructs one to 'learn to find cuts, thrusts and slices.' Other manuals, such as Jorg Wilhalm Hutter's, depict techniques connected to these actions which are not described in this or the following sections. I argue that this drill is designed to help a student learn to bind, wind, and thrust at the sword, while feeling their opponent's actions, and begin to take creative steps in their own fighting. This leads naturally to Ringeck's next section, which introduces sparring to the students. This drill serves to teach the principles described by Ringeck in the first paragraph and by Liechtenauer in his attendant *Merkverse*, perhaps more than as a specific set of techniques which will form a major part of the style. I will attempt to lay out specific techniques in two drills exploring two of the soundest possibilities that cover the major ways that Ringeck's description can play out. The goal of these is to learn the principles of *Vor, Nach, Indes*, weak, strong, the capability to sense these things, and apply your techniques correctly against a resisting opponent.

A winding technique called the '*Edel Krieg*,' or 'Noble War,' appears in the *Krumphau* section. It is used to defeat an opponent who has used a *Krumphau* against you, exploration of this technique lies beyond the scope of this volume. The name of the technique is strikingly similar to the name Ringeck uses for these techniques here. I believe that the two techniques are the same technique, and therefore much of the instruction given there is also relevant here and vice-versa. There Ringeck says to bind strongly with the sword, move the hands up, and work with the point in front of your head with winding techniques.

Krieg, as it is described here, has at least two possible variations that fit Ringeck's description, and I believe that the evidence from the sources in the Liechtenauer tradition indicates that room exists within the style for variation beyond what is literally stated in the text. Both interpretations I offer will be the same up to the first winding. The contingent point is what is meant by the word '*versetzen*.' This word usually functions as a general term which I understand as a rough equivalent to the word 'parry.' There are two major contingent points in this technique where this word comes up: 'When he parries the thrust' referring to the thrust from the winding, and 'If he follows your sword to parry,' each of them have multiple possibilities. The way you translate *versetzen* will lead you to the variations possible. The fact that Ringeck, Hutter, and Kal do not precisely agree in their text or illustrations establishes two additional points. First, that there are strong grounds for variation at this stage. Second, that there was not necessarily agreement among the masters of this tradition as to what to teach for this technique, or how to teach it.

Theory: the Paulus Kal interpretation

Paulus Kal shows a very clear version of *Krieg* that gives us a rough match for Ringeck's text, and he connects it to the lines from Liechtenauer's language in Lesson 12 where he says 'if he notices it, take him low'. Kal's illustration shows the last stage of an exchange in which the attacker uses the *Zornhau*, is parried with a *Zornort*, the attacker then uses *Winden*, and then the defender uses a bad parry, moving their sword directly to the side without threatening the attacker. The attacker then uses *Durchwechseln* from left *Ochs*, and stabs a lower quarter. He implies that if the thrust is parried again in a similar fashion, then the attacker can do another *Durchwechseln*. This could be repeated until the defender is struck.

While it matches the text I object to using this interpretation exclusively as a teaching tool for this section because if the opponent ever executes a good parry that threatens us, they will break the cycle, and we must respond with other techniques. This makes it hard to teach profitably at this early stage, because *Durchwechseln* is a very risky move requiring a clear read of an opponent's mistake. I also object because this kind of parry, which fails to threaten the opponent, does not exist in this tradition as something that the student is intended to learn, only as a mistake they can exploit. Ringeck specifically warns against doing this kind of parry in the opening sections. Thus, Kal's version will only prove useful as a way to fight an opponent who has made the mistake of fighting your sword. In addition, teaching this technique requires the person in the role of the teacher to have sufficient experience to not develop bad habits while practicing it. This means that the person in the role of the defender should not be a comparatively new student, which can be impractical in modern groups. Fourth, you cannot learn a great deal in practicing this technique as it is not broadly applicable, and it certainly doesn't help a great deal for learning *Vor*, *Nach*, and *Indes*. After the first winding the student might become weak in the bind, but will never be in the *Nach*. I include it here for one reason, it seems to also be Jorg Wilhalm Hutter's first image of *Krieg*, and it would build naturally from the interpretation of Kal in the previous sections.

Hutter's *fechtbuch*, by comparison, gives us a very large section on *Krieg* from folio 5r clear through till folio 8v, much of which is not repeated anywhere else in the tradition as far as I know, and may be considered either as original material, or as extrapolations of Liechtenauer's original teachings, or merely a broader presentation of the teaching method of Liechtenauer. Hutter connects the following portion of the *merkverse* 'Learn to find Cuts, Thrusts, and Slices' to his section on *Krieg*. Hutter does not, however, give us a gloss matching Ringeck's instructions. It seems likely that his sections on *Krieg* show the results of creative work at this point in the manual. Probably, what Hutter shows include the results of sparring matches, and drills developed from there, which he found helpful for his students. Most of these, however, bear little resemblance to common modern practice, or to the text of other manuals, including Ringeck's.[39]

Now, I want to clarify something. I do in fact think that this version of the technique should be taught, just that it fits better later in the curriculum in the section on *Durchwechseln*. If you teach it here, then I believe you should also use other variations for *Krieg*, and you should not pair newer students together to learn it. I do not think that this version of the technique is incredibly helpful for newer students commencing their training, especially since if everyone in your group learns Ringeck thoroughly the parry shown in Kal will never be done in your group's sparring, and they will seldom use it. I include this technique here because it is the most easily documented method with accord between the sources.

Drill: Paulus Kal's *Krieg*

Begin from out of distance. Approach and have the attacker strike a *Zornhau*. The defender executes a *Zornort*. The attacker winds against it. The defender does a bad parry setting the point aside without threatening the attacker and seizing the *Vor*. The attacker senses this and while remaining in the winding uses *Durchwechseln*, withdrawing their point down toward them until they can clear the opponent's sword and attempt a thrust to the lower quarter. The defender does another bad parry and the attacker changes through again from the other side to thrust to the lower opening again. These last moves may be repeated until the defender is struck. While this move can be done on both sides it works noticeably better from left *Ochs*.

Ben attacked with a *Zornhau*, Randy defended with a *Zornort*, Ben has now wound against Randy's blade. Randy senses he is weak in the bind and must respond.

Randy panics and uses a bad parry withdrawing his point and parrying Ben's thrust to his left. Ben senses that he is now weak in the bind, but that Randy is not threatening him.

Ben uses *Durchwechseln*, lowering his point so his blade can travel to the other side of Randy's sword.

Ben now threatens a thrust to Randy's lower quarter.

Randy once again uses a bad parry, preventing the thrust and becoming strong in the bind, but failing to make a credible threat, leaving Ben free to attack again.

Ben uses *Durchwechseln* again, lowering his point beneath Randy's sword, and he will thrust to Randy's left opening.

Ben finishes the *Durchwechseln*, thrusting to Randy's upper left opening. This sequence may be repeated until Randy is struck.

Theory: Ringeck's *Krieg*

In this second version of *Krieg* I have interpreted this technique to include more dynamic winding with the intention of fluidly moving the student into the next section where they learn 'to find cuts, thrusts and slices' according to Ringeck's instructions.

We already know that Ringeck differs considerably from Dobringer, Kal and Hutter on several points. In this section I will proceed on the assumption that they taught different interpretations of this technique, or that the teachings and techniques for this section were intentionally fluid, and allowed for variation.

I developed my interpretation of *Krieg* by drawing on the illustration of the second position from Jorg Wilhalm Hutter's section on *Krieg*, his connection with the following section 'Learning to Find Cuts, Thrusts, and Slices,' the Glasgow version of Ringeck's illustration of the reverse grip during a *Durchwechseln*, the Goliath manual's depiction of the *Mutieren*, and the *Durchwechseln* from Ringeck's description of the *Kurtzhau*, 'Short Strike,' from the *Krumphau* section, which describes a special form of *Durchwechseln* designed to facilitate a winding, and thrust to the face, while remaining in contact with the opponent's sword, rather than disengaging completely as is usually shown with the *Durchwechseln*. All the building blocks of this interpretation come from the Liechtenauer tradition's source material. As much of it as possible comes from Ringeck's own books, and I feel it matches the principles and concepts of Ringeck's previous teachings and his larger style, strategy, and pedagogy, much better than Kal's or Hutter's illustrations.[40]

Again, the crucial point of interpretation is what does he mean by the word *Versetzen* when it is used against the *Winden*. I examined the counters that Ringeck and the broader Liechtenauer tradition offer us. The clearest action taught that has a countermeasure with an attack to a lower target is the *Mutieren*. So here I interpret the '*Versetzen*' as the opponent winding against our winding to threaten us with a *Mutieren* like that shown in the Goliath manual.[41]

In order to parry a *Mutieren*, and follow the text's instructions to 'remain in the winding and thrust to the lower opening' you will need to employ a reverse grip with the off hand, and move the sword in front of your right shoulder, such as that shown in the Glasgow manual's image for *Durchwechseln*.[42] This will allow you to remain in the winding with your right arm curled, just in a more extreme manner than usual, to cover the right quarters with your own *Mutieren*. Your footwork will prove crucial to making this technique work. If you close the distance with a lateral step, and stab to the lower quarter, you will also protect your exposed opening. You will need to aim your thrust to the left leg, hip, belly, or groin and step past your opponent's point.[43]

If your opponent 'follows your sword' they will again '*Versetzen*', and in this case I interpret this as winding to right *Pflug*. The attacker may then counter this with a special *Durchwechseln* that winds under the opponent's weak. I modeled this technique on the *Kurczhau Durchwechseln*, from the *Krumphau* section of the Dresden version of Ringeck's manual. You do this *Durchwechseln* by retracting your point to parry the thrust, bringing your strong into contact with their weak, and then bringing your point up, and slightly to the side, so that their point slides up to your strong. When your point is aimed at your desired target, you thrust. Please note, this works if the thrust from *Pflug* is aimed at the upper quarters, where the heart and lungs are, but if it is aimed at the lower quarters another action, such as *Abnemen*, will need to be used instead, and it is appropriate to teach your students to break this drill with *Abnemen* after they have gotten the hang of working in the bind.

The defender can then respond with another *Mutieren*. The drill then repeats these last motions from the *Mutieren*, until one fighter is struck, or until someone decides to break the pattern with Abnemen or other technique.[44]

This interpretation also has the advantage of remaining at the sword the entire time, which serves to build feeling skills as the students flow back and forth between *Vor* and *Nach* throughout the drill. While it is best taught by a competent teacher all the defender in the drill needs to know is how to do is a *Mutieren* and a winding to *Pflug*. Your group should be confident in their control before they attempt this non-compliantly because thrusts are more accident prone than cuts, especially if aimed at the face. Remain vigilant, and start slow, but work up to a high level of speed and resistance.

One disadvantage to this interpretation is that it can only be done on one side. You cannot easily enter a reverse grip winding from a right *Ochs*, or a left *Ochs* if you are left-handed. Left-handed people can easily practice this against a right-handed opponent, but the techniques will need to be done from the other side if a left-handed person is the attacker.

Remember, Ringeck seems to present *Krieg* in connection with the following section on finding cuts, thrusts and slices, and serves to teach feeling the bind and fighting Indes more than a specific technique or set of techniques to learn. This interpretation serves as a primer for creative use of the longsword and a primer to sparring. In practice the drill will rarely play out past three or four actions, and leaving the drill for creative solutions should be encouraged after the group has learned the drill's primary form.

Drill: Ringeck's *Krieg*

The attacker will have the role of the student, and the defender will have the role of the teacher. The attacker and defender start from well out of distance. The defender calls attack. The attacker approaches and executes a *Zornhau* from their right to the opponent's upper left quarter (reverse sides if the attacker is left-handed). The defender parries with a *Zornort*. The attacker winds against it. The defender winds to a *Mutieren* at the lower right opening. The attacker takes a step, whether it should be a simple step, passing step, or otherwise depends on the precise positioning and there is considerable room for variation. The attacker changes their grip to the reverse grip pushing their sword in front of their right shoulder and aiming their own *Mutieren* to the lower opening. The defender parries this by winding to a lower right *Pflug*. The attacker executes a special *Durchwechseln*, by retracting their point to become strong in the bind and winding to threaten the defender's upper left quarter. This sequence may be repeated from the *Mutieren* until someone is struck.

Ben will attack and take on the role of student, Randy will defend and take on the role of teacher.

Ben approaches and attacks Randy parries with a *Zornort*, threatening a thrust to Ben's face.

Ben winds against the thrust, threatening Randy's face.

Randy executes a *Mutieren* over Ben's *Winding* threatening a thrust to Ben's lower right quarter.

Ben switches to a reverse grip, pushing the sword in front of his upper right quarter to parry Randy's *Mutieren* with a *Mutieren* of his own and takes a passing step forward with his left leg to minimize the threat of Randy's thrust.

Ben takes a passing step back and winds to right *Pflug* threatening a thrust.

Ben feels Randy's winding and executes a special *Durchwechseln*. He retracts his point just enough to become strong in the bind and allow him to wind to Randy's next opening.

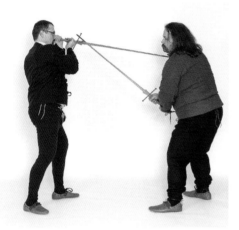

Ben uses the leverage of the reverse grip to wind his sword to threaten Randy's face.

Randy attempts a second *Mutieren* against Ben's winding. This picture shows how he goes over Ben's blade.

Randy completes his second *Mutieren*.

Ben uses a simple step to execute his reverse grip *Mutieren* and thrust to Randy's leg. This sequence of actions from the first *Mutieren* on may continue repeating until one or the other training partner is struck. As you progress you will find it often helpful to leave the sequence to deliver a cut, *Duplieren*, or other technique.

Lesson 16: Finding Cuts, Thrusts, and Slices

In all winding learn to find cuts, thrusts, and slices.
  You must feel if you should Cut, Thrust, or Slice.
  When winding you must feel whether you should cut, slice or thrust. Thus you will know which of the three options is best. You are not to cut if you should thrust; not to slice, if you should cut; and not to thrust if you should slice. Focus, and if he parries one attack then hit him with another. Thus: If your thrust is displaced, cut instead. If he comes in under your sword slice from below against his arm.
  Always consider these principles in every fight; if you want to achieve the skill of the masters who face you. (The Dresden Manuscript)

Theory: finding cuts, thrusts, and slices

The primary lesson of this section concerns feeling in the bind. What you do when you are in the moment should be dictated by the situation you perceive in the very moment that you need to act. Pre-planning can lead to the wrong technique, but neither should you wait till you can visually see your opponent's openings. You must develop an instinct and sensitivity using your sense of touch, guided by the drills and teachings of Liechtenauer and Ringeck. Only through time, effort, patience, and no small number of bruises can get you the experience you need to become skilled at this.

The text here on the surface tells you merely to execute the same techniques that you would in the previous drills. The difference is that now you have many different options and an unstructured situation. Your job as a student is to learn to see the situations and match the correct technique to them. Then the next step is to turn it into an instinct.

This concept is one you will come back to again and again and again over the years as you pursue mastery of this art. You should make sure that you set aside time to practice this in depth frequently as you learn new techniques.

Theory: slice against the arm

At this point Ringeck introduces a technique which he will not return to for a significant time. The hand/forearm slices of the Liechtenauer tradition serve as the primary counter to grappling in this fighting style. They are only rarely depicted, but it is no coincidence that they are first introduced here long before the other grappling techniques. They hold two chief advantages over using grappling to defeat grappling. First, they are easier to execute and teach, which makes them immediately accessible to a beginning fighter. Second, they are often more decisive because they can seriously wound or maim the opponent, causing them to retreat or flinch so that they may be defeated with a clean strike or thrust.

The preparation to grapple almost always involves raising the sword to deflect the point of the opponent's weapon. Therefore the first slice taught is the slice that comes from below. This is all Ringeck and Liechtenauer teach about how to counter an opponent who attempts to close and grapple with you until much later in the manual. Spend a great deal of time teaching this technique because it will be the primary method your students use to deal with these devastating kinds of attack for a very long while. They will rely on it. While Ringeck and Liechtenauer treat this as a fight-ender, it may also be very helpful to teach them to execute an additional *Zornhau*, or other technique, at the end of the drill.

Method: slice against his arm

In this drill you should execute the *Zornhau* drill as normal, but one of the partners, ideally a skilled teacher, should attempt to rush in and grab the other person or their weapon to disarm or throw them. This is, by design, more free-form than the previous drills because the students must learn to sense the decision to close and grapple. They should also be aware that this is typically done by someone who is at a disadvantage when remaining at the sword, and is an alternative to *Winding* or Abnemen when the distance is very close.

The person defending against the grapple must be on the lookout for the moment when the grappler lifts their sword up to deflect their own point and begins to move in. At that moment they should disengage from the bind and press their long edge forcefully against the grappler's arms, sliding either forward or backwards to let the edge do the work. It is often advisable to use hand protection for this training as the hands and wrists are the primary target. If the hands are close together, as for example in a pommel strike, then the student should move the strong and hilt of their sword low and slice across the hands or wrists. Be careful not to catch your cross on your opponent's arms. If the hands are widely separated the student should slice the hand that is trying to take the grip of them as long as it will also control the sword. If the student fails to slice the teacher should take the student's balance or with students who have more experience and can fall safely, throw the student.

There are many ways to grapple with an opponent. I will show just two here to serve as examples. Expose your students to many grappling attacks and help them find ways to counter them with hand slicing. It is very helpful to teach and review correct falling technique at the beginning of each such lesson to ensure that the students are not injured.

Drill: slice under the arm against a pommel strike

Pommel strikes are the easiest close technique to counter with hand slices because it presents the hands high and forward. As such they are an ideal place to start new students. The teacher will assume the role of the attacker, and the student the role of the defender. The attacker approaches and steps very close as they strike against their student. When the student defeats their attack with a *Zornort* at close distance the attacker will lift their sword and step in close to strike at the face with the pommel.

The defender will be learning to sense this, and bring their sword down and under the attacker's arms and press their long edge up and into their wrists or hands. With adequate hand protection this should be done forcefully. As contact is made the blade should be pushed or pulled against the hands, wrists or forearms, to simulate the slicing action. After executing the slice, step away from the opponent, and execute an *Abnemen*, or other technique, to finish the fight. If the attacker feels the slice happen correctly, they should stop their own motion at that moment and allow the *Abnemen* to happen. Should the defender fail to execute the slice the attacker should demonstrate their pommel strike.

Begin from out of distance.

Ben attacks and Randy parries with a *Zornort* at very close range.

Ben takes a second passing step forward, deflecting Randy's point by lifting his sword and bringing the pommel up to strike toward Randy's face.

Randy counters the pommel strike by stepping back and slicing at Ben's hands with his long edge.

Randy presses his long edge up against Ben's hands.

Drill: slicing against a grappling

Begin as above, but with no set attacker or defender, but do select a teacher and a student. Ideally, the teacher will be experienced at grappling with a longsword. The teacher's job will be to find opportunities to execute grappling and throws, in an effort to give the student opportunities to feel how, where, and when to slice in order to counter these many different techniques. Even though Ringeck presents a fairly small number of these, there are many possibilities, and what we hope to do here is train instincts more than individual techniques. We will show just one example below.

Ben attacks and Randy attempts to parry with a *Zornort* but the range is too close.

This time Ben decides to attempt throw Randy. He releases his hilt with his right hand. He sets aside Randy's sword by lifting his left hand and letting his sword hang down and to the right to protect him from direct actions from Randy's blade.

If Ben succeeds, he will set up a throw over his forward leg by stepping behind Randy's front leg and using his right arm across Randy's chest to pull him over.

To prevent this Randy extends the distance as Ben comes in and slices at Ben's exposed sword hand. He will need to be cautious as Ben might be able to do something with his sword, but he has at the very least gained a significant advantage.

Method: teaching students to find cuts, thrusts and slices

To develop the creative, aggressive, seeking mind that a fighter in this style should display, the key training tool should become sparring, punctuated by drill training to perfect technique. I recommend leaving the drills behind for a while, and letting your group learn how to really fight *Indes*. I recommend dedicating a long time to sparring and letting your students learn their lessons by earning a lot of bruises.

Tips for teachers: sparring

One of the most important things you can do at this stage is to let go of the need to constantly correct what the students do. Wait and see if they will correct it themselves before stepping in to make them do more drills. Hopefully, they will begin to take a more active hand in their own learning. When they lose in sparring ask them if they understand what they did wrong and how they might have won.

Lesson 17: The Four Openings

On the four openings

There are four openings to know
Strike wisely
In all engagements
Do not let how he acts make you hesitate

Gloss: Mark the four openings on the man which you shall fight at. The first are on the right and left sides above the belt. The other two are the right and left sides below the belt. To take the openings, carefully decide which you should come against as you approach the fight. Skillfully work against the openings, thrust in with the Long Point, use Nachraisen, and all other techniques you wish to try. Do not worry about what he is up to. Fight wisely. Skillfully employ the strike you think is best, and by doing so you will prevent his techniques from threatening you. (The Dresden Manuscript)

Theory: know the Four Openings

This section provides some masterful advice reprising some of Liechtenauer's fundamental teachings. They advocate an aggressive mindset, focusing our thinking on how we will attack our opponent. Perhaps most importantly he follows this with a word of caution that we should attack in a manner that prevents our opponent from threatening us. We use our attacks to control our opponent until we have defeated him.

Ringeck introduces here two terms that bear some additional explanation, Long Point and *Nachraisen* (Pursuing). Long Point is simply the position that a thrust naturally ends in, where we have extended our arms and sword towards, and ideally into, our opponent. He specifically mentions thrusting into this position, it may be done from *Ochs* after a *Winding*, or the more instinctive *Pflug* position with the sword point up in front of us. The reasoning for introducing Long Point here seems to be a point about finishing the motion of our thrusts skillfully, i.e. in a manner that controls the opponent's sword or otherwise forces a response from them that will not endanger us.

The second term, *Nachraisen*, may be translated as 'pursuing,' 'pursuit,' 'chasing,' 'giving chase,' or more literally as 'travelling after.' Ringeck seems to have reserved a complete training regimen in *Nachraisen* until after the other four strikes and the four guards have been taught and synthesized. In this fighting style *Nachraisen* means to exploit either a hesitation on the part of our opponent, or a critical miscalculation of distance in their attack with our own attack during the time they have left themselves vulnerable. There are many ways to perform *Nachraisen*: it is a principle of action, as much or more than it is a technique, or set of techniques. At this point, rather than teach *Nachraisen*, which has its own section much later in the manual, we will simply teach that if as we enter distance our opponent hesitates we should strike our *Zornhau*, and our opponent strikes from much too far away so that they miss, and this action brings them into distance, we should, again, strike our *Zornhau* at them. Full training in *Nachraisen* lies beyond the scope of this volume.

Here Ben stands in right *Ochs* with his upper left opening exposed. If he uses an extreme back-weighted stance his front leg could become a valid target, but the upper opening should generally be preferred as the longsword can better protect you as you attack when you aim for these.

Ben stands in right *Pflug*, which covers his lower right opening, but does not, technically, cover either of his upper openings. In most stances the lower openings are actually significantly farther away and harder to hit than the upper openings, and these are, therefore, not good places for an initial attack. Because the blade and stance are oriented to his right side, he can quite easily defend his upper right quarter. This makes his upper left his most vulnerable quarter.

Drill: attacking *Ochs*

Ochs is the most difficult guard to attack with a *Zornhau*. This drill will help acclimate the students to having some openings closed off when they approach an opponent. Have the defender stand in *Ochs*. The attacker and the defender shall approach from out of range. Once they have reached appropriate striking range, the attacker shall strike the exposed opening with a *Zornhau*. They will need to use footwork to step around the point and minimize their exposure to a direct thrust as they do this. Change to the other *Ochs* and repeat. If the defender uses an extreme back-weighted stance a *Zornhau* at the forward leg may be the correct move.

Drill: 'Seeing openings'

The attacker and the defender will begin well out of distance. The defender starts in *Alber* and abruptly shifts into an *Ochs* or *Pflug* position as the attacker closes distance. The attacker must choose the correct footwork and attack for the new position. As the lesson progresses the defender should begin in different positions, change to other positions at the last moment, and attempt to use evasive footwork. The goal is to teach the attacker to correctly choose which opening to attack as the situation changes. Eventually you should consider adding positions not found in Liechtenauer, and those used with other weapon systems, especially those with bucklers and shields so the student can become aware of the fluid nature of their opponent's openings.

Method: attacking left *Ochs*

Left *Ochs* naturally defends the *Zornhau* from the right. It is the most difficult position to attack with a *Zornhau* if you are right-handed. Attacking this position requires an attack at the quarter opposite the natural side. More importantly the threat of a thrust to face or chest can make this quite intimidating. Ringeck later teaches how to use a *Krumphau* to attack the hands when the opponent stands in *Ochs*, but learning how to use a *Zornhau* to defeat this is important at this stage in a student's training.

Randy enters distance against Ben, who is standing in left *Ochs*, preventing Randy from cutting from his right.

Randy cuts a *Zornhau* at Ben's upper right quarter. To do so he takes an aggressive gathering step with his left foot. This requires a strong adjustment with his right foot as well.

Drill: striking at left *Ochs*

Most people will naturally cut from their right, and need to work hard to cut well from their left when facing a point from *Ochs*. Have the receiver of the technique stand with their longsword in left *Ochs*, covering the line that *Zornhaus* from the right side travel on. They should aim their point directly at their training partner's face so that it is difficult to see how long the weapon is. Have the person practicing their cut approach and attack the opponent's upper right opening with a *Zornhau* from the left.

Drill: striking at left *Ochs*

Most people will naturally cut from their right, and need to work hard to cut well from their left when facing a point from *Ochs*. They should aim their point directly at their training partner's face so that it is difficult to see how long the weapon is. Have the person practicing their cut approach and attack the opponent's upper right opening with a *Zornhau* from the left.

Lesson 18: *Duplieren* and *Mutieren*

The Text and the Gloss about Duplieren, Mutieren, and how they break the four openings.

   If you will reckon how to skillfully break the four openings Dupliere above and Mutiere below.

   Truly, not even masters will be safe.

   If you have learned this well, your opponent will not even be able to make his own strikes.

When you wish to skillfully break the four openings Duplieren to the upper openings against the strong of his sword, and Mutieren to his other opening. I tell you truly, he will not be able to protect himself, nor use his own strikes or thrusts. (The Dresden Manuscript)

Theory: the role of *Duplieren* and *Mutieren*

These techniques provide a way to break the cycle of cutting, feeling, winding and cutting again. *Duplieren* offers a harassing attack to the upper openings, slicing at the face or head, which we hope will cause the opponent to flinch so we can apply a more powerful technique. *Mutieren* attacks the lower openings with a thrust, and while less deadly than a thrust to the face or chest, damaging the major organs in the belly, groin, and legs can put an opponent out of commission through structural damage and pain, and the internal injuries and bleeding can kill given enough time. A thrust through leg muscle or the lower abdomen can put an opponent out of commission quite quickly, but it should be treated as less likely to stop an opponent than the first techniques taught.

   Lindholm posits that the last paragraph of this section depicts a technique rather than advice about the general employment of these techniques. I allow that this is possible, though Ringeck does not explain a sequence for how to do these techniques in tandem, so teaching a drill to chain them together at this point makes little sense. I prefer to think of this paragraph as general advice about the use of these techniques, and the effect it will have on the opponent.

   The line '*If you have learned this well, your opponent will not even be able to make his own strikes*' indicates several things important about the entirety of Ringeck's art, as well as these specific techniques for breaking the four openings. First, Liechtenauer and Ringeck developed an art centered on the principles of how to attack and how to respond to a defense so that we can continue to attack. Second, in any bind one will either be weak or strong. In either case a thoroughly educated and practiced fighter in this style will always be able to apply one of the techniques they have learned, and, theoretically, should be capable of beating any attack by following the principles of this art. This creates confidence in the fighter.

By learning these techniques and relying on these principles you will always have a ready answer to any attack. Third, this perspective and preparation helps you seize the *Vor* and keep it. A fighter of this style thinks like a hunter going after dangerous prey, looking for openings and taking them. *Duplieren* and *Mutieren* provide more ways to keep your opponent reacting to your techniques until he makes a mistake and you beat him.

As for *Duplieren* and *Mutieren* specifically, these techniques are not so frequently able to end a fight outright as other techniques, but they do, however, provide exceedingly swift ways to seize the *Vor*, especially in a confined space such as in a low-ceilinged indoor area or on a crowded battlefield. The swiftness of *Duplieren* makes a hit extremely likely if your opponent's upper openings are vulnerable. While a tick slower than conventional *Winding* to the face, *Mutieren* will injure the lower quarters, significantly slowing your opponent, possibly causing them to fall, or even preventing them from being able to fight at all, all while controlling their sword to keep you safe.

Lesson 19: *Duplieren*

When you use a Zornhau, or any other Oberhau, and he parries it strongly, then, in that very moment, thrust the pommel of your sword under your right arm and strike him with crossed hands at the sword behind his blade between the sword and the man. Aim the blow across the mouth, or strike him on the head with this technique. (The Dresden Manuscript)

Theory: *Duplieren*

Duplieren serves as a more aggressive, but less immediately lethal, alternative to winding. The name literally translates as 'doubling', but it might be better translated as 'doubling over,' or 'folding,' in the sense that 'doubled over' is used in English or '*verdoppelt*' in modern German.

Ringeck mentions two principal means of executing the *Duplieren*. Tobler and Lindholm interpret *Duplieren* as a slice across the face with the long edge from left to right initiated after a typical *Zornhau-Zornort* exchange and the lateral parry with crossed hands. This matches the first description in Ringeck's text well, and I heartily agree with this.[45] I wish to add some comments about the range it should be executed at. If done from too far away, then we rely completely on our opponent being so distracted by the slice to do anything to us. *Duplieren* needs a strong, tight, motion, at a relatively close distance, in order to keep you safe after the slice is delivered. Ideally, you should get close enough with the crossed-hands defense that thrusting becomes inconvenient or impossible. At the correct distance. this long edge slice becomes an excellent technique, and can strike quite hard.

In Paulus Kal's manual we see what I believe is the 'hit him on the head' version of the *Duplieren*. The executor of the technique, who stands on the left-hand side of his illustration, seems to have used a passing step at very close range. They use their strong and cross to deflect their opponent's point up and away from themselves as they thrust their left hand forcefully under their right arm and strike the opponent on the crown of their head with their point, or their short edge in an *Ochs* position on their right.

Both *Duplieren* are classified as *Schnitten* (slicing) in the original German. Ancient swordsmen did not design the technique to cleave the enemy's head in two, but to distract them with pain and a threat to sensitive areas. *Duplieren* will seldom end a fight, or deliver a lethal blow in and of itself. You must, therefore, follow a *Duplieren* with a thrust or cut. Because of the presence of helmets *Duplieren* works less well in a sparring match than it would in real life.

Fortunately, *Duplieren* sets up many excellent follow-up techniques very well, including: *Zornhaus* and *Zwerchhaus* to the upper or lower quarters, *Abnemen*,

Zucken followed by cuts to the head, *Mutieren* to the lower openings, grappling, *Durchwechseln*, and *Nachraisen* can all easily work, depending on the position the opponent adopts after the *Duplieren*. The trick is to train so that you can perceive the vulnerable opening, and do a devastating follow-up technique, depending on the exact range and position.

   Duplieren's threat to the eyes and face make it more dangerous than usual to practice with. You should not do *Duplieren* practice, other than ideal forms drills, without helmets.

Drill: *Duplieren* across the face

The attacker and defender start well out of distance. The attacker approaches and strikes a *Zornhau*. The defender counters with a *Zornort*. When the attacker senses that they are becoming weak in the bind, they thrust the pommel under their right hand with their left hand, pushing the defender's blade to their left with the strong of their sword, preventing the attacker from making their *Zornort* connect. Then the attacker should pull or push the long edge of their sword across the defender's face aiming, ideally, for either the eyes or

Ben approaches and attacks with a *Zornhau*, Randy responds with a *Zornort*.

Ben, sensing that he is weak in the bind, thrusts his left hand under his right hand, deflecting Randy's thrust to his left and setting up his slice to Randy's face.

Ben draws his long edge across Randy's eyes to harass and distract him.

Randy flinches, raising his hands to cover his face.

Seeing that Randy is open Ben does a small *Durchwechseln* and stabs Randy in the chest.

mouth to force the opponent to flinch. As they do this, they should make a very fast step forward, or possibly to the side, to remove the threat of a thrust. As the defender flinches or tries to control your blade then aim a cut or thrust to the next opening they present. This action should be accompanied by another small quick step out to the side to gain a better angle.

Drill: *Duplieren* with pushing slice

In this drill after crossing our hands we will push our long edge across our opponent's face, aiming for the eyes or mouth. Once we land the slice we will feel and see how the opponent responds, and use a more devastating cut or thrust to finish the fight.

From the *Zornort* Ben will thrust his left hand under his right to deflect the *Zornort*.

Here Ben thrusts his left hand under his right deflecting the thrust and setting him up to push his edge across Randy's mouth.

Randy flinches, covering his face by raising his arms.

Seeing Randy flinch, Ben presses his long edge against Randy's hands, which will prevent him from being able continue using his weapon.

Drill: Paulus Kal *Duplieren*

The attacker approaches and attacks with a *Zornhau* from the right. The defender counters with a *Zornort* from the right. The attacker passes forward with the left foot as they execute the *Duplieren*. The attacker should thrust their left hand forcefully under their right and lift their sword somewhat up and forward. As they do this, they should rake their point across the defender's face, or hit them on the head with the short edge. If the attacker is close to the defender, they should wind to an extended forward *Ochs* while pressing the sword forward and to the left to deflect the defender's point. If you are not particularly close, then keep your hands in front of you as you wind the weapon. Do not lift your weapon away from the opponent's point and leave yourself open. Follow this with a cut or thrust to the lower opening as prudent.

Ben attacks and Randy parries with a *Zornort*.

Ben executes Kal's *Duplieren* to strike Randy on the head with his short edge. He takes a passing step to his left, catching Randy's point with his strong and cross.

Randy flinches and, lifting his sword, exposes his lower opening.

Ben begins a *Zwerchhau* to strike Randy's lower opening.

Here we see Ben's *Zwerchhau* making contact with the lower opening near the groin and pelvis.

Here we see the follow-through position such a cut would end at.

Lesson 20: *Mutieren*

Mark the Mutieren

If you bind against his sword, with an Oberhau, or other technique, wind the short edge at his sword, raise your arms, hang your sword over his sword and thrust at his lower opening. Use this from both sides. (The Dresden Manuscript)

Theory: *Mutieren*

Ringeck describes the *Mutieren* as a technique which can deal with a wide variety of situations, essentially any bind at the sword where the lower opening is left vulnerable. It can be done from any bind in which you are weak, but, if the illustrations are any indication it's primary use seems to have been to counter a winding to the upper quarters from *Ochs*. It can 'therefore' also function as an alternative to *Abnemen*.

While aiming a thrust at the lower targets is less deadly and less likely to stop an opponent cold, *Mutieren* achieves two things. It makes it more difficult for your opponent to *Zucken* or *Abnemen*. It also makes it harder for them to simply maintain the dominant position. They will often need to employ complex windings, such as those shown in the *Edel Krieg* section, to deal with it in the bind. I find it particularly helpful when your opponent is winding. The other advantage of *Mutieren* is that it is more compact than cutting from the bind. This could be very helpful if you are dealing with a low ceiling, or a tight formation.

As far as iconography is concerned only a few images appear in the corpus of the tradition, the Goliath image, the image from Paulus Kal, and two images in Hutter showing the technique done on both sides. The Goliath depiction fits Ringeck's description better than the depiction in Paulus Kal, which seems to show the person who is strong in the bind underneath aiming for the lower quarter having caught the weak of their opponent's sword on their long edge. Hutter shows no binds at all, which may mean that he is not actually trying to show a version working in practice but the idea that Mutieren is simply any thrust ot the lower opening.

Entering the position shown in Paulus Kal's illustration, simply does not work from the *Oberhau* on *Oberhau* bind under normal circumstances, or any of the techniques shown thus far. The most common way I've seen to enter the position Kal shows is either countering a *Durchwechseln* or a low *Zwerchhau*. Neither of these make much sense in the context of the techniques previously taught. The *Zwerchhau* has not been introduced yet, and an opponent using *Durchwechseln* when you were set up to threaten with your point can only be attributed to a colossal error in judgement. It is possible that Kal's image has an artistic error and does not properly show which sword is on top at the point where they cross. He has other errors in his art, such as on his page depicting the *Krumphau* where the hand is placed impossibly behind the elbow. If there is an error, then Paulus Kal may actually be showing a nearly identical position to the Goliath image.

Method: executing *Mutieren*

When an opponent winds from a *Zornhau* on *Zornort* bind you also wind so that your blade goes over their sword. You will have to bring the sword far enough to the side so that your strong will land on their weak, which will prevent attacking the upper quarter. Aim your sword's point down toward their belly, groin, or leg and thrust.

Drill: *Mutieren*

Begin from out of distance. The attacker approaches and strikes a *Zornhau*. The defender parries with a *Zornort*. The attacker uses *Winden*, winding their sword into an *Ochs* on their left. The defender then applies *Mutieren*, winding over the attacker's winding and thrusting to the lower openings. Aim the point at the belly, loins, or leg.

Ben attacks and Randy parries with a *Zornort*.

Ben winds against Randy's thrust.

Randy begins to wind over Ben's blade as he begins his *Mutieren*.

Randy finishes the wind over Ben's sword and thrusts to his lower opening.

Method: permutations

Follow-up maneuvers from these techniques aren't explained in the manual. I believe this is because they depend a great deal on what your opponent leaves open. A *Mutieren* to the leg might not disable an opponent, a *Duplieren* alone will not defeat an opponent by itself, but whether and where you should attack will depend on what the position is. Follow-up techniques will be required in most scenarios. Personally, I find the *Zwerchhau*, *Zornhau*, *Edel Krieg*, and *Zucken* to be the best such techniques, and I suggest that you open up the drill to creative variation and sparring once the students have clear proficiency with these techniques so that they can experiment with follow-up techniques. Have them spar a great deal with these techniques added into their repertoire.

Tips for teachers: sparring with *Mutieren*

You should have the group spar in several different ways, with different numbers of hits and rule sets in order to extend the development of your ability to read your opponent's openings and execute your techniques accordingly.

As we end this section, I would suggest spending a great deal of time working on these techniques and sparring with them. Make them instinctive so that you can learn how to incorporate them in your style.

Conclusion

Isaac Newton once said, 'If I have seen further, it is by standing on the shoulders of giants,' and he was not even the originator of the metaphor. I hope my work will be of value. I have put a great deal of time and effort into writing this book, but I frankly acknowledge the work that has been done by so many scholars and martial artists in the modern age whose previous labors have made my contribution possible. More importantly, I am exceedingly grateful that Sigmund Ringeck wrote his manuscript, that Johannes Liechtenauer developed his fighting style, and to the scholars and masters who copied and preserved their works, at not inconsiderable expense.

My chief hope is that I might have been able to reproduce, with as few nods to modern sensibilities and capabilities as possible, not only their techniques, but their training method. I believe that their mindset and pedagogy greatly influenced the outcome of their training. I took as my model the oldest martial arts I could find record of, which seemed as close to the form of Ringeck's as I could find, and compared those with the writings and art I hoped to interpret. I have become acutely aware of how easy it is to accidentally introduce foreign concepts, which may sometimes be useful, but which in fact, do not belong to the art I am trying to recreate.

I do not believe that my work is without flaw or foreign interpolation, despite my best efforts to make it so. Ringeck's text's age, fragmentary nature, ambiguity, and lack of illustrations make it impossible to use in complete isolation. My goal was never to create the 'ultimate longsword style', but to recreate Ringeck's as closely as I could, because I believed that he and Liechtenauer already came as close as humankind can come to that goal. I doubt that I could add much to their art, but I hope the insights I've gleaned from studying it these last twenty years might be of use to other students of historical European martial arts.

Thank you for reading my work. I invite you to send me your feedback, and I hope you will contact me with your ideas, questions, and criticisms. It is my hope that the next volumes, and hopefully the second editions after them, will be improved by the input of other inquiring minds. I also hope that I have been able to add something to your own practice and appreciation of Ringeck's longsword style, and historical European martial arts more broadly.

I salute you.

Appendix

Suggested School Rules

Because this book attempts to establish a clear pedagogy and method for teaching, I felt it might be helpful share our school rules. Some of the elements in these suggested rules and etiquette depend on a formal school setup, and others will not fit the preferences of a particular group. You will need to adjust these accordingly.

The 'at ease' position referred to in these rules is taken from my observation of historical European source material. Variations can be seen in a wide range of iconography and in several manuals including Talhoffer's and Paulus Kal's. You place your weapon point up at your shoulder in a position which is very vertical with your hilt close to your body to keep it out of the way. This also avoids blunting or dirtying the weapons on the ground, as well as endangering your training partners. This position also has the advantage of being very close to the *Vom Tag* position, and is easy to strike from if necessary.

The Code of Conduct of the Hilt and Cross

1. You are responsible for your training partner's safety and shall always endeavor to keep them safe. Our training partner is kept safe by our self-control. Accidents are symptoms of poor training and control, and we will not tolerate them.
2. We will use our art only to defend our lives, our loved ones, our fellow beings, and our freedoms.
3. Obey the Instructor promptly.
4. Never enter an area being used for training. If you must cross through an active practice area, either wait for a break in practice, or alert the training people and wait for their acknowledgement before crossing.
5. The school safe word is 'Halt!'. If a problem arises shout 'Halt!' as loudly as you can. When you hear 'Halt!' called, freeze in the exact position you are in and look around before moving.
6. Treat your training weapon like a real weapon. When you are not using your weapon hold it 'At Ease.'
7. Salute your training partner when beginning and ending a set of exercises.
8. Do not talk during a lesson. If you have a relevant observation or question raise your hand and wait for acknowledgement.

9. Always practice with the intent to be able to use the techniques you learn as its creators would have.

10. Do not deviate from assigned or agreed upon activities. Do not experiment with new ideas during time that has already been dedicated to other activities. Time will be dedicated to experimentation. You may always take a minute out during a lesson to write down relevant insights and plans for future practice if you wish.

11. Never show disrespect to any student, instructor, officer, staff member, or visitor to the school. Interested persons are welcome to watch.

12. Do not handle equipment that does not belong to you without the express and immediate permission of the owner. If equipment is damaged while you are using it, you will be required to replace it or reimburse the owner.

13. We claim the right to challenge, and be challenged by, other martial artists to show our skills and test theirs. We will always answer an equitable challenge. We will do so respectfully and cordially. We will not gloat in victory, or make excuses in defeat. We will seek to learn, and, when asked, to teach, in every such encounter. If we challenge another martial artist, or accept a challenge ourselves, we shall do so with the utmost respect and formality, with no desire to cause them harm.

15. We acknowledge the necessity and limitations of competition as both a historical and modern practice for creating effective martial arts and martial artists. We will not center our practice, or our teaching on it. We reject uncontrolled, suicidal, and de-contextualized practices, even if they are rewarded in competitive environments.

16. Wear appropriate school attire.

17. Embrace a strict code of honesty. Answer all questions forthrightly. Do not attempt to answer questions you do not know the answer to. If you do not know the answer to a question refer the asker to someone who knows, and admit that you do not know.

18. Test new ideas thoroughly, and honestly attempt to discover if there is validity and value in them.

Notes

Introduction

1. For evidence of this one can look at almost any work on the subject from the period to see how they present this art being practiced and taught. See the books below for examples.

   Anonymous. MS. Germ. Quart. 2020 (5879), *The Goliath*. Biblioteka Jagiellonska Kraków. 1510–1520.

   Codex Wallerstein, Cod. I.6.4º.2, Universitätsbibliothek Augsburg in Augsburg, Germany.

   Döbringer, Hanko, translated and edited by Lindholm, David. *Hanko Dobringer's fechtbuch from 1389*, Cod.HS.3227a. Germanisches Nationalmuseum, Nürnberg, 2005.

   dei Liberi, Fiore, Francesco Novati editor. *Flos Duellatorum*. Pissani-Dossi edition; Bergamo; acquired 1902, dated 1410.

   Kal, Paulus. Cgm 1507, Bayern 1462; Bibliotheca Palatina Mannheim; Bayerische Staats Bibliothek.

   Hutter, Jorg Wilhalm, Liechtenauer, Johannes. Cod.I.6.20.2. Universitatsbibliothek, Augsburg, Germany, 1523.

   Ringeck, Sigmund. MS Dresd.C.487 Sächsische Landesbibliothek, Dresden, Germany, 1504-1519.

   Ringeck, Sigmund. Fecht und Ringerbuch MS E.1939.65.341. Germany. 1508. Glasgow Museums Scotland.

   Ringeck, Sigmund. Rostock, fechtbuch zu Ross und zu Fuss, MS Var.82. Universitätsbibliothek Rostock, Rostock, Germany.

   Pseudo Peter Von Danzig. Fechtbuch Peter von Danzig zu Ingelstat. MS 3227a, Germanisches Nationalmuseum, Nurembug Germany. Also, Codex Danzig Cod.44.A.8 Biblioteca dell'Accademia Nazionale dei Lincei e Corsiniana in Rome, Italy.

   Talhoffer, Hans, translation and editing by Rector, Mark. *Medieval Combat: A Fifteenth-Century Manual of Swordfighting and Close-Quarter Combat. Talhoffer fechtbuch: Gerichtliche und andere Zweikampfe darstelland, Anno Domini 1467*. VS-Books, Heren Germany, Carl Schulze & Torsten Verhulsdonk, 1998, Greenhill Books, 2000.

   Vadi, Phillipo. *De Arte Gladiatoria Dimicandi*. MS Vitt. Em. 1324 (1482-1487). Biblioteca Nazionale Centrale di Roma, Italy.

   Vadi, Phillipo. *De Arte Gladiatoria Dimicandi*. Spada Press, 2017.

   Wilhalm, Jörg. *Fechtbuch Jörg Wilhalm*. Cgm 3712. Bayerische Staatsbibliothek Munich, Germany.

2. Talhoffer, Hans, *Talhoffer's fechtbuch: Gerichtliche und andere Zweikampfe darstelland*, 1467, translated and edited by Mark Rector, *Medieval Combat: A Fifteenth-Century Manual of Swordfighting and Close-Quarter Combat* Greenhill Books, London, Stockpole Books, Pennsylvania, 2000. On plates 33–67 and 77–78 Talhoffer depicts techniques

using half-swording, wrestling, murder strokes (striking with the pommel and hilt to bludgeon or hook the opponent), and close-range thrusting, all of which can apply directly or be easily adapted to armored combat. Talhoffer actually devotes more space to this material than he does to techniques where the sword is held normally.

3. Skoss, Diane, editor, *Koryu Bujutsu: Classical Warrior Traditions of Japan, Vol. 1*, Koryu Books, Berkeley Heights NJ, 1995.

—— Armstrong, Hunter 'The Koryu Bujutsu Experience,' pgs. 19-38.

Skoss, Diane, editor, *Sword and Spirit: Classical Warrior Traditions of Japan, Vol. 2*, Koryu Books, Berkeley Heights NJ, 1997.

—— Keely, Liam, 'The Tojutsu of the Tatsumi-ryu, Murphy's Law and the K.I.S.S. Principle,' pgs. 111-150.

—— Friday, Karl F., 'Kabala in Motion: Kata & Pattern Practice in the Traditional Bugei,' pgs. 151-170.

—— Tsuneo, Nishioka, 'Uchidachi & Shidachi,' pgs. 171-177.

Skoss, Diane, editor, *Keiko Shokon: Classical Warrior Traditions of Japan, Vol. 3*, Berkeley Heights NJ, 2002.

—— Keely, Liam, 'Interview with Nitta Suzuyo: Headmaster of the Toda-ha Buko-ryu,' pgs. 63-86.

—— Beaubien, Ron, 'Challenges in Observing the Koryu Bugei,' pgs. 87-108.

—— Bodiford, William M. 'Soke: Historical Incarnations of a Title and its Entitlements,' pgs. 129-144.

—— Amdur, Ellis, 'Renovation and Innovation in Tradition,' pgs. 145-178.

—— Bristol, George H. 'The Professional Perspective: Thoughts on the Koryu Bujutsu from a United States Marine,' pgs. 179-194.

Draeger, Donn F., *Comprehensive Asian Fighting Arts*, Tokyo and New York, Kodansha International, 1980.

Draeger, Donn F., *The Martial Arts and Ways of Japan, Volume 1: Classical Bujutsu*, Weatherhill, New York & Tokyo, 1973.

Draeger, Donn F., *The Martial Arts and Ways of Japan, Volume 2: Classical Budo*, Weatherhill, New York & Tokyo, 1973.

Draeger, Donn F., *The Martial Arts and Ways of Japan, Volume 3: Modern Budo & Bujutsu*, Weatherhill, New York & Tokyo, 1974

Draeger, Donn F., *The Weapons and Fighting Arts of Indonesia*, Charles E. Tuttle Company, Rutland, Vermont, USA, Tokyo, Japan, 1972.

Lorge, Peter, *Chinese Martial Arts: From Antiquity to the Twenty-First Century*, Cambridge University Press, Cambridge, New York, 2012.

The evidence of training methods for ancient warriors gives us a wide variety of activities that they underwent, including: solo form training, strength training, unit maneuvers, archery, horseback archery, wrestling, other forms of unarmed fighting, as well as training in each and every weapon system used by the warriors in question. I say here in my book that the heart of their training was the individual drills, typically between teacher and student, because without this the execution of all of the other training methods will suffer. Unit tactics make little difference if, once contact is made with the enemy the persons in contact cannot do the techniques which will inflict violence, at a personal level. Strength training will only improve one's combat ability if it improves the strength of the body in the right ways and to the right levels. Solo form training will be of little more value than regular physical exercise unless the motions are well understood, the actions clear, the purpose of each movement intuitive, and the role of each technique integrated in the mind of the student within the larger system. This knowledge can only really be taught in drills and sparring with a proficient teacher. All ancient fighting styles I have researched, from before the middle of the 17th century, have at their root this training method where a teacher guides a student through their development. The strategy may be simple or complex, the movements few or numerous, the weapons for military or civilian use, but where a competent teacher is available these kinds of knowledge can be assimilated much more easily, which is not to say that they are easy to learn, just orders of magnitude easier with an excellent teacher.

Chapter 1

4. The only real clues we have to Ringeck's life history are the brief mentions of his service to his patron Duke Albrecht of Bavaria and Count Palatine of the Rhine and Paulus Kal's inclusion of a Sigmund Amring, whose name echoes the variations of Ringeck's name which appear in other versions of his manual, in the list he presents of members of the Society of Liechtenauer.
   Ringeck, Sigmund, MS Dresd.C.487 Sächsische Landesbibliothek, Dresden, Germany, 1504-1519, pgs. 10v-11r.
   Kal, Pualus, Cgm 1507, Bayerische Staatsbibliothek in Munich, Germany, 1470~, pgs. 2r.
5. Chidester, Michael, 'A Big-Picture Look at the fechtbuch Tradition', lecture at the Iron Gate Exhibition, Washington DC, 2012.
6. The evidence for this can be taken from the lists of weapons taught which occur in a number of *fechtbucher*, the compiling of source material in the books that include these books, and the appearance of sections teaching the use of these weapons within these sources. All of the primary sources from the Liechtenauer tradition provide substantiation for this assertion.
7. Chidester, Michael, 'A Big-Picture Look at the Fechtbuch Tradition', lecture at the Iron Gate Exhibition, Washington DC, 2012.

Chapter 2

8. Amdur, Ellis, "Koryu Meets the West," in Skoss, Diane, editor, *Koryu Bujutsu: Classical Warrior Traditions of Japan*, Vol. 3, Koryu books, Berkeley Heights NJ, 1997.
   Amdur, Ellis, "Renovation and Innovation in Tradition," in Skoss, Diane, editor, *Sword and Spirit: Classical Warrior Traditions of Japan, Vol. 2*, Koryu Books, Berkeley Heights NJ, 1997.
   Lowry, Dave, "Promise and Peril: The Potential of Following Multiple Koryu," in Skoss, Diane, editor, *Keiko Shokon, Classical Warrior Traditions of Japan, Vol. 3*, Koryu Books, Berkeley Heights NJ, 2002.
9. Jager, Eric, The Last Duel: *A True Story of Crime, Scandal and Trial by Combat in Medieval France*, Broadway Books, 2005. This book offers us a good example of an exception to this general pattern. In the eponymous duel Carrouges seems to have thrown le Gris to the ground, put him in a front mount, and beaten his helmet with his sword's blade, hilt, or pommel, until the latch broke, and then after some additional grappling, drawn his dagger, and after attempting to force a confession, slain le Gris by stabbing him in the head. Please note that, even though this example includes considerable groundwork, that Carrouges still ended the fight with a dagger, and that application of the weapons was the chief goal of the

groundwork. Thus, even when there was groundwork in the historical knightly arts, we can clearly see that it differed greatly from modern groundwork in competitive martial sports.

10. Ringeck, Dresden Version, pgs. 13r - 17v.
    Dobringer, pgs. 18v – 21r.

11. Camargo, Arturo, 'Taking Great Pains in Your Knightly Practices,' HROARR Website, accessed at http://hroarr.com/article/take-great-pains-in-your-knightly-practices-a-brief-review-of-medieval-and-renaissance-training-methodologies/, 2016, accessed April 2018.
    Cartier, Mike, 'The Art of Control: Fechtschule Manifesto Parts I and II,' Meyer Freifechter Guild Website, https://sites.google.com/site/mffgusa/academics, 2011, accessed April 2018.
    Clements, John, 'Using the F-word -- The Role of Fitness in Historical Fencing,' The ARMA Website, http://www.thearma.org/essays/fit/RennFit.htm#.WsoujC-ZMWo, 2005, accessed April 2018.
    Duarte, Dom King of Portugal, *The Royal Book of Jousting, Horsemanship, and Knightly Combat: A Translation Into English of King Dom Duarte's 1438 Treatise*, Chivalry Bookshelf, 2010.
    Martens, Krist, 'Towards a New Approach in HEMA Tournaments: Let's Fence Naked!' HROARR, http://hroarr.com/article/towards-a-new-approach-in-hema-tournaments-lets-fence-naked/, 2014, accessed April 2018.
    The core training method described by Ringeck of course seems to be partner practice in pre-arranged forms. All of my inferences about sparring in this system are just that, inferences from oblique statements in the text and from other evidence from the time period. Every Medieval and Renaissance manual on swordsmanship I have ever read describes or provides illustrations of this kind of pre-arranged practice using real or training swords. While gloves are rare they do show up in some manuals, such as in I.33. In any case Sigmund Ringeck, Fiore dei Liberi, George Silver, Jorg Wilhalm Hutter, and hosts of others describe this kind of training. Many other kinds of training also show up in historical source material. Sparring is evidenced by the massively popular tournaments of Medieval and Renaissance Europe and certain phrases in certain particular sections of the manuals from the martial traditions of the era, some of which will be addressed in this volume from Ringeck directly. In Johannes de Sacrobosco's *Da Sphaera Mundi* which was owned by the Sforza family and dated to approximately 1460, making it roughly contemporary with Ringeck we find the painting named 'Children of the Sun' which shows partner drill training, or possibly sparring, wrestling, weight lifting, acrobatics, and possibly solo training with various weapons. We see considerable evidence of vigorous exercise by men of the day including forms practice, sparring in armor, and even climbing walls.

Chapter 3

12. Bartosz Sieniawski, 'The Saber's Many Travels,' HROARR Website, http://hroarr.com/article/the-sabers-many-travels-the-origins-of-the-cross-cutting-art/, 2013, accessed April 2018.
    Galas, Matt, 'Russian Test Cutting Practices,' HROARR Website, http://hroarr.com/article/russia-test-cutting-practices/, 2012, accessed April 2018.

Chapter 4

13. Camargo, Arturo, "Taking Great Pains in Your Knightly Practices," HROARR Website, accessed at http://hroarr.com/article/take-great-pains-in-your-knightly-practices-a-brief-review-of-medieval-and-renaissance-training-methodologies/, 2016, accessed April 2018.

Cartier, Mike, "The Art of Control: Fechtschule Manifesto Parts I and II," Meyer Freifechter Guild Website, https://sites.google.com/site/mffgusa/academics, 2011, accessed April 2018.

Clements, John, "Using the F-word – The Role of Fitness in Historical Fencing," The ARMA Website, http://www.thearma.org/essays/fit/RennFit.htm#.WsoujC-ZMWo, 2005, accessed April 2018.

Duarte, Dom King of Portugal, *The Royal Book of Jousting, Horsemanship, and Knightly Combat: A Translation Into English of King Dom Duarte's 1438 Treatise*, Chivalry Bookshelf, 2010.

Martens, Krist, "Towards a New Approach in HEMA Tournaments: Let's Fence Naked!" HROARR, http://hroarr.com/article/towards-a-new-approach-in-hema-tournaments-lets-fence-naked/, 2014, accessed April 2018.

The core training method described by Ringeck of course seems to be partner practice in pre-arranged forms. All of my inferences about sparring in this system are just that, inferences from oblique statements in the text, and from other evidence from the time period. In the places where Ringeck instructs us to develop creativity, I interpret these as places where we introduce and use sparring as a teaching tool, and this is according to my own experience as a martial artist.

Every Medieval and Renaissance manual on swordsmanship I have ever read describes, or provides illustrations, of this kind of pre-arranged practice using real or training swords. While gloves are rare, they do show up in some manuals, such as in I.33. In any case Sigmund Ringeck, Fiore dei Liberi, George Silver, Jorg Wilhelm Hutter, and hosts of others describe this kind of training. Many other kinds of training also show up in historical source material. Sparring is evidenced by the massively popular tournaments of Medieval and Renaissance Europe, and certain phrases in certain particular sections of the manuals from the martial traditions of the era, some of which will be addressed in this volume from Ringeck directly. In Johannes de Sacrobosco's *Da Sphaera Mundi* which was owned by the Sforza family, and dated to approximately 1460, making it roughly contemporary with Ringeck, we find the painting named "Children of the Sun" which shows partner drill training, or possibly sparring, wrestling, weight lifting, acrobatics, and possibly solo training with swords, staffs, and wrestling. We see considerable evidence of vigorous exercise by men of the day including forms practice, sparring in armor, and even climbing walls.

14. The invention of modern safety gear for training is a little fuzzy, but the invention of the fencing mask is chiefly attributed to Antoine Texier La Boëssière, who taught in the latter half of the eighteenth century. While some rare historical examples of tournament gear that vaguely resembles modern tournament armor do exist, they appear rarely and are much more rarely referenced, which makes the likelihood of their widespread use slim. I believe it is probably the case that such things were adopted by individuals or relatively isolated groups, but that the ideas never caught on because of the same issues that we face today. The Metropolitan Museum of art has one such

helmet dated to 1450-1500 from Germany which they connect to the von Stein family of Swabia, though oddly they do not directly connect it with any of the known martial arts traditions, but rather equestrian sports.

Training weapons, and in the case of the subject of this particular book, training longswords are much more common. We see the characteristically British example of the waster, and of course steel training swords are depicted frequently with, and are deeply connected to, the Liechtenauer tradition.

Cartier, Mike, 'The Art of Control: Fechtschule Manifesto Parts I and II,' Meyer Freifechter Guild Website, https://sites.google.com/site/mffgusa/academics, 2011, accessed April 2018.

Kokochashvili, George and Shalva, *Innovation and Inventions in Fencing*, accessed http://www.academia.edu/7140535/Innovations_and_Inventions_in_Fencing, 2014, accessed April 2018.

Norling, Robert, 'The Whatchamacallit-Schwert,' HROARR Website, 2013, accessed April 2018.

Metropolitan Museum of Art Website, Tournament Helm, https://www.metmuseum.org/art/collection/search/24678, accessed April 2018.

15. 'Kendo.' Wikipedia. https://en.wikipedia.org/wiki/Kendo, accessed Dec 2018.

16. See notes 1–3, See also the deer skin leather gauntlets used in several of the koryu such as Yagyu Shinkage Ryu. Kendo equipment was invented in the late 1680s nearly a century after the battle of Sekigahara when Japan had been at peace for two full generations.

17. My claim here about the sophistication of later sword styles will undoubtedly prove controversial, but take for example Henry Angelo's manual for British military saber fencing, comparing it to Ringeck the techniques have fewer permutations, nor are they well distinguished by a clear objective in a combat situation. He sets up little in the way of context, and many of the defenses would be considered outright mistakes in Ringeck's system because of the ease with which a proficient swordsman can defeat or ignore them. This might be taken as a stylistic difference, but I do not think so. The nuances of controlling distance and timing which might make such actions appropriate, are not explained. Nor do we see extensive teaching with closing actions, grappling, disarms or instructions on how to prevent or deal with these actions. They show no instruction in the use of companion weapons, or how to deal with them. Accounts of the effects of British cutting in the era lead me to conclude that it was inconsistent, whereas accounts of Russian and Polish cutting are impressive. A far simpler explanation than those of the apologists for the British systems is that a lesser degree of expertise was expected of the officers being trained, and the same was expected of their opponents. Limited training time, the need to train massive numbers of officers with a very small number of proficient swordsmen, and the lesser need to use their swords in battle, dueling, or self-defense pushed the style in these directions.

Gevaert, Bert, 'The Use of the Saber in the Army of Napoleon, Parts I-IV,' HROARR Website, https://hroarr.com/article/the-use-of-the-saber-in-the-army-of-napoleon-part-i/, https://hroarr.com/article/the-use-of-the-saber-in-the-army-of-napoleon-part-ii/, https://hroarr.com/article/the-use-of-the-saber-in-the-army-of-napoleon-part-iii/, https://hroarr.com/article/the-use-of-the-saber-in-the-army-of-napoleon-part-iv-wounds-caused-by-the-saber/, accessed 2019.

Galas, Matt, 'Russian Test Cutting Practices' Oct 22, 2012, HROARR Website, https://hroarr.com/article/russia-test-cutting-practices/, accessed 2019.

Bartosz Sieniawski, 'The Saber's Many Travels,' HROARR Website, http://hroarr.com/article/the-sabers-many-travels-the-origins-of-the-cross-cutting-art/, 2013, accessed April 2018.

Marsden, Richard, *The Polish Saber: The Use of the Polish Saber on Foot in the 17th Century*, Tyrant Industries, 2015.

18. Galas, Matt, 'Russian Test Cutting Practices' Oct 22, 2012, HROARR Website, https://hroarr.com/article/russia-test-cutting-practices/, accessed 2019.

Chapter 6

19. Fiorato, Veronica, Boylston, Anthea, and Knusel, Christopher, *Blood Red Roses: Archaeology of a Mass Grave from the Battle of Towton AD 1461*, 2nd ed., Oxbow Books, 2007.

Keegan, John, *The Face of Battle*, London, Jonathan Cape, 1976.

Tracy, Larissa and DeVries, Kelly editors. *Wounds and Wound Repair in Medieval Culture*. Brill, 2015.

Chapter 7

20. Vadi, Phillipo, *De Arte Gladiatoria Dimicandi*, MS Vitt. Em. 1324 (1482-1487), Biblioteca Nazionale Centrale di Roma, Italy, page 27v.

Galas, Matt, IGX 2018 Lecture: Historical Rule Sets in HEMA by Matt Galas. Youtube, https://www.youtube.com/watch?v=No-LRK5UXBE&t=24s, accessed 2018.

Galas, Matthew, 'Historical Rule-Sets,' The HEMA Alliance Project, HEMA forums, http://hemaforums.com/viewtopic.php?t=664, 2010, accessed 2018.

Chapter 10

21. Many manuals show evidence of this kind of grip maintaining space between the hand and the cross, and while modern practice of the *Zwerchhau* and *Scheilhau* specifically often has people place their thumb on the flat of the blade, or in its fuller, if their weapon has one, we see in the original manuals a different kind of grip. For evidence from Ringeck himself the Glasgow version of Ringeck shows this kind of grip throughout, especially on pages: 1v, 2r, 2v, 3v, 4v, 5r, 6r, 7r, 9v, 10r, 13v, 14r, 14v, 15r, 16r, and 19v. We also see it in MS. Germ. Quart. 2020 (5879), also known as the Goliath Manual, throughout its entire longsword section including the pages dealing with the Zwerchhau and Schielhau. The Munich version of Paulus Kal's fechtbuch shows this on pages: 58v, 60r, 61v, 62r, 62v, 66r, 67v, and 68v. The Solothurner version of Paulus Kal's manual (Cod.S.554) shows this on a similar variety of pages throughout its longsword section. Even later manuals such as Meyer's, which do show the hand pressed against the cross in some images, particularly those with the thumb on the flat, show this kind of grip such as the left figure of the top right pair in illustration B, the right figure of the center pair and the left figure of the top left pair in illustration C, the left figure of the front pair in illustration D, the left figure of the top left pair, the left figure of the center pair, and the left figure of the top right pair in illustration E, the left figure of the top left pair in image F, and both front figures, as well as the left figure of the top

left pair, in illustration H. Considering the breadth of the evidence, and the fact that it helps the cross protect the hands I use this as the default grip, making adjustments where called for. For examples of the variety of grips used by ancient swordsmen see the following images:

Dei Liberi, Fiore, *Fior di Battaglia,* MS Ludwig XV 13, J. Paul Getty Museum, Los Angeles CA, pages 20r-21v.

Kal, Paulus, Paulus Kal Fechtbuch, Cgm 1507, the Bayerische Staatsbibliothek in Munich, Germany, pages 52v-57r.

Talhoffer, Hans, *Talhoffer's fechtbuch: Gerichtliche und andere Zweikampfe darstelland,* 1467, translated and edited by Mark Rector, *Medieval Combat: A Fifteenth-Century Manual of Swordfighting and Close-Quarter Combat* Greenhill Books, London, Stockpole Books, Pennsylvania, 2000, 3v.

'The Goliath Manual,' MS Germ. Quart. 2020, Biblioteka Jagiellonska, Krakow, Poland, written circa 1510, 19v, 21r.

22. Burton, Francis, *Book of the Sword*, Dover publications, revised ed., 2012 (originally published 1884). Burton mentions that swordsmen of his day preferred a toothier edge, but again this is only ancillary evidence from a much later period than the one interpreted in this book. Nor has any research been done to substantiate the effectiveness of this or how specifically sharp they kept their swords.

23. George Turner's essay 'Sword Impacts and Motions: An Investigation and Analysis' offers a simple explanation of the basic physics of the larger sword motions and the physics of generating power in the strike with a European sword. While it is not perfect, nor complete, I strongly recommend that all practitioners of HEMA read it so that they can understand some of the elementary physics behind the way swords work. It can be found on the website of the Association for Renaissance Martial Arts at: http://www.thearma.org/spotlight/GTA/motions_and_impacts.htm. I will deliver his conclusions in brief in the following paragraphs.

The pommel's purpose is twofold. It changes the location of the forward pivot point of a sword. The forward pivot point is the place at which an object naturally rotates when force is exerted upon it from a particular location, in this case the part of the grip close to the hilt where your sword-hand goes. Though his sample size was quite small, he concluded from the strong correlation of forward pivot points between the swords he examined that this was one of the goals of sizing, shaping, and attaching a pommel to the weapon separately from the construction of the blade was to control the position of the forward pivot point to the purchaser's liking. He demonstrates mathematically that while changing the center of gravity happens in the process, it is a by-product, not the goal, of attaching the pommel. He argues that this is so because it is entirely possible for two swords of the same length and general size and shape to have the same center of gravity, but totally different pivot points. In other words, finding out where the center of gravity is will not tell you how a weapon will behave in your hand. Ancient sword makers used pommels to control the location of forward pivot points, and add power to a strike, not to control the location of centers of gravity, even though these are related.

This would have been particularly important if one was facing an opponent wearing high quality mail, in which case, a cut which uses a more efficient drawing motion, such as those we see in Northern India and Japan, would be rendered almost totally ineffective. Considering that mail was worn on battlefields well into the 1500s and sometimes even the 1600s, and that in times of strife men might wear a mail shirt under their outer garments, using a cutting technique which helps deal with mail by delivering more force is simply a logical way to do things. I recommend that people who question the effectiveness of historical mail as armor observe the pin demonstration in Dirk H. Breiding's presentation 'How to Mount a Horse in Armor and other Chivalric Problems' from the Metropolitan Museum of Art's Youtube channel. The demonstration can be found around the nine minute mark. Please note that most modern reproductions of mail do not compare well with historical mail either in ring design or the quality of their construction, and many testers currently neglect adding a gambeson or other backing materials under mail which was, in the era of the longsword, nearly always used with this form of armor.

Turner, George, 'Sword Impacts and Motions: An Investigation and Analysis,' Website of the Association for Renaissance Martial Arts, http://www.thearma.org/spotlight/ GTA/motions_and_impacts.htm, accessed 2006.

Geißler, Robert, 'Concerning the Dynamics of Swords.' HROARR Website, http:// hroarr.com/article/concerning-the-dynamics-of-swords/. 2014 accessed April 2018.

Breiding, Dirk H., 'How to Mount a Horse in Armor and other Chivalric Problems,' Metropolitan Museum of Art's Youtube Channel, The Met, https://www.youtube.com/ watch?v=NqC_squo6X4, Published 2010.

The General Teaching

24. Kaeuper, Richard. *Chivalry and Violence in Medieval Europe*. Oxford University Press, Oxford, 1999.

    Jager, Eric, *The Last Duel: A True Story of Crime, Scandal and Trial by Combat in Medieval France*, Broadway Books, 2005.

    Jackson, Diedre, *Medieval Women*. The British Library, London, 2015.

    Levin, Carole, *The Heart and Stomach of a King: Elizabeth I and the Politics of Sex and Power*, University of Pennsylvania Press, 2nd ed. 2013.

    Morrison, Susan Signe, *A Medieval Woman's Companion: Women's Lives in the Middle Ages*. Oxbow Books, 2015.

    Ward, Jennifer, *Women in Medieval Europe, 1200-1500*, Pearson Education Ltd., 2002.

    Weisner-Hanks, Merry E., *Women and Gender in Early Modern Europe*, New Approaches in European History, Cambridge University Press, 3rd ed., 2008.

25. Ibid.

26. Chandler, Jean, 'Butchers, Bakers, and Candlestick Makers,' Lecture presented at Boston Sword Gathering VIII, 2016.

    Chidester, Michael, 'A Big Picture Look at the fechtbuch Tradition,' Lecture presented at Boston Sword Gathering VIII, 2016.

27. My rendering of Ringeck's text departs deliberately on the basis that his use of the word 'wechsel' in this instance seems to be short for '*Durchwechseln.*' It is consistent with his previous teachings about striking to the head and the body and the dangers of *Durchwechseln*. Hutter uses the full word '*Durchwechseln*' in this portion of his version of the *Zedel*, which lends weight to this interpretation. Hutter, Jörg Wilhalm, *Jörg Wilhalm*

Hutter Kunst zu Augspurg, Cgm 3712, Bayerische Staatsbibliothek Munich, Germany, pg. 2r.

28. Ringeck, Glasgow, folio 15v.
29. Von Danzig, Codex Danzig Cod.44.A.8, page 13v.
30. Von Danzig, lists the leg as a target for second and third permutations, http://wiktenauer. com/wiki/Nuremberg_Hausbuch_(MS_3227a), accessed April 2018. Pseudo Peter Von Danzig. Fechtbuch Peter von Danzig zu Ingelstat. MS 3227a, Germanisches Nationalmuseum, Nuremburg Germany.
31. Bartosz Sieniawski, 'The Saber's Many Travels,' HROARR Website, http://hroarr.com/ article/the-sabers-many-travels-the-origins-of-the-cross-cutting-art/, 2013, accessed April 2018.
    Galas, Matt, 'Russian Test Cutting Practices,' HROARR Website, http://hroarr.com/ article/russia-test-cutting-practices/, 2012, accessed April 2018.
32. Meyer, 57.
33. Fiore Getty version, 23r-a.
34. Meyer, 41, 57, 60-61.
35. Von Danzig, lists the leg as a target for second and third permutations, http://wiktenauer. com/wiki/Nuremberg_Hausbuch_(MS_3227a), accessed April 2018. Pseudo Peter Von Danzig. Fechtbuch Peter von Danzig zu Ingelstat. MS 3227a, Germanisches Nationalmuseum, Nurembug Germany.
36. Wallerstein, Cod.I.6.4., page 3v.
    Kal, Munich version page 60r.
    Ringeck, Dresden, 21r-21v.
37. Paulus Kal Fechtbuch MS 1825, folio 20v.
38. Hutter, Cgm 3711, Bayerische Staatsbibliothek in Munich, Germany, folio 5r - 8v.
    Kal, Paulus. Cgm 1507, Bayern 1462; Bibliotheca Palatina Mannheim; Bayerische Staats Bibliothek. Folio 60v.
39. Ibid.
40. Wallerstein, Cod.I.6.4., page 3v.
    Kal, Munich version page 60r.
    Ringeck, Dresden, 21r-21v.
41. Ibid., and Goliath manual Mutieren page 17v.
42. Fiore, Morgan Transcription, Stance of the Anvil, 13-d.
    Ringeck, Sigmund, MS E.1939.65.341, Folio 15v, Glasgow Museums, Glasgow Scotland.
    Talhoffer, plate 1.
    Goliath, 13r, 19v, 21r, 29r.

43. Wallerstein, Cod.I.6.4., page 3v.
    Kal, Munich version page 60r.
    Ringeck, Dresden, 21r-21v.
    Hutter, Cgm 3711, Bayerische Staatsbibliothek in Munich, Germany, folio 5r - 8v.
44. Anonymous. MS. Germ. Quart. 2020 (5879), *The Goliath*. Biblioteka Jagiellonska Kraków. 1510–1520. pgs. 17v.
45. Ringeck, Glasgow, folio 5r.

Bibliography

Primary sources

Angelo, Henry. *Rules and Regulations for the Infantry Sword Exercise, 1817*. Printed and Sold by William Clowes, Northumberland-court Strand. 1817.

Anonymous. MS. Germ. Quart. 2020 (5879), *The Goliath*. Biblioteka Jagiellonska Kraków. 1510–1520.

Burton, Francis. *The Book of the Sword*. Dover Publications, revised ed. 2012 (originally published 1884).

Döbringer, Hanko, translated and edited by Lindholm, David. *Hanko Dobringer's fechtbuch from 1389*, Cod.HS.3227a. Germanisches Nationalmuseum, Nürnberg, 2005.

dei Liberi, Fiore, Francesco Novati editor. *Flos Duellatorum*. Pissani-Dossi edition; Bergamo; acquired 1902, dated 1410.

Hutter, Jorg Wilhalm, Liechtenauer, Johannes. Cod.I.6.20.2. Universitatsbibliothek, Augsburg, Germany, 1523.

Kal, Paulus. Cgm 1507, Bayern 1462; Bibliotheca Palatina Mannheim; Bayerische Staats Bibliothek.

Ringeck, Sigmund. MS Dresd.C.487 Sächsische Landesbibliothek, Dresden, Germany, 1504-1519.

Ringeck, Sigmund. Fecht und Ringerbuch MS E.1939.65.341. Germany. 1508. Glasgow Museums Scotland.

Ringeck, Sigmund. Rostock, fechtbuch zu Ross und zu Fuss, MS Var.82. Universitätsbibliothek Rostock, Rostock, Germany

Ringeck, Sigmund. MS Dresd.C.487 Sächsische Landesbibliothek, Dresden, Germany, 1504-1519.

Pseudo Peter Von Danzig. fechtbuch Peter von Danzig zu Ingelstat. MS 3227a, Germanisches Nationalmuseum, Nurembug Germany. Also, Codex Danzig Cod.44.A.8 Biblioteca dell'Accademia Nazionale dei Lincei e Corsiniana in Rome, Italy.

Talhoffer, Hans, translation and editing by Rector, Mark. *Medieval Combat: A Fifteenth-Century Manual of Swordfighting and Close-Quarter Combat. Talhoffer fechtbuch: Gerichtliche und andere Zweikampfe darstelland, Anno Domini 1467*. VS-Books, Heren Germany, Carl Schulze & Torsten Verhulsdonk, 1998, Greenhill Books, 2000.

Wilhalm, Jörg. *fechtbuch Jörg Wilhalm*. Cgm 3712. Bayerische Staatsbibliothek Munich, Germany.

Vadi, Phillipo. *De Arte Gladiatoria Dimicandi*. MS Vitt. Em. 1324 (1482-1487). Biblioteca Nazionale Centrale di Roma, Italy.

Vadi, Phillipo. *De Arte Gladiatoria Dimicandi*. Spada Press, 2017.

Codex Wallerstein, Cod. I.6.4º.2, Universitätsbibliothek Augsburg in Augsburg, Germany.

Secondary sources

Amdur, Ellis, 'Renovation and Innovation in Tradition,' in Skoss, Diane, editor, *Sword and Spirit: Classical Warrior Traditions of Japan, Vol. 2*, Koryu Books, Berkeley Heights NJ, 1997.

Anglo, Sydney. *Chivalry in the Renaissance*. Boydell Press, Woodbridge, 1990.

Anglo, Sydney. 'How to Kill a Man at Your Ease: Fencing Books and the Dueling Ethic.' in *Chivalry in the Renaissance*. Boydell Press, Woodbridge; 1990.

Anglo, Sydney. *The Martial Arts of Renaissance Europe*. Yale University Press, New Haven and London, 2000.

Armstrong, Hunter. 'The Koryu Bujutsu Experience,' in Skoss, Diane, editor. *Koryu Bujutsu: Classical Warrior Traditions of Japan, Vol. 1*. Koryu Books, Berkeley Heights NJ, 1995.

Barber, R. and Barker, J.R.V. *Tournaments: Jousts, Chivalry and Pageants in the Middle Ages*. Woodbridge, 1989.

Barker, J.R.V. *The Tournament in England, 1100–1400*. Woodbridge, 1986.

Beaubien, Ron, 'Challenges in Observing the Koryu Bugei,' in Skoss, Diane, editor. *Keiko Shokon: Classical Warrior Traditions of Japan, Vol. 3*. Berkeley Heights NJ, 2002.

Bodiford, William M. 'Soke: Historical Incarnations of a Title and its Entitlements' in Skoss, Diane, editor. *Keiko Shokon: Classical Warrior Traditions of Japan, Vol. 3*. Berkeley Heights NJ, 2002.

Bristol, George H. 'The Professional Perspective: Thoughts on the Koryu Bujutsu from a United States Marine,' in Skoss, Diane, editor. *Sword and Spirit: Classical Warrior Traditions of Japan, Vol. 2*. Koryu Books, Berkeley Heights NJ, 1997.

Broekhoff, Jan. 'Chivalric Education in the Middle Ages.' in Zeigler, Earle ed. *Sport and Physical Education in the Middle Ages*. Trafford Publishing, Victoria 2006.

Chidester, Michael. 'A Big-Picture Look at the fechtbuch Tradition,' Lecture at the Iron Gate Exhibition, Washington D.C., 2012.

Draeger, Donn F. *The Martial Arts and Ways of Japan, Volume 1: Classical Bujutsu*. Weatherhill, New York & Tokyo, 1973.

Draeger, Donn F. *The Martial Arts and Ways of Japan, Volume 2: Classical Budo*. Weatherhill, New York & Tokyo, 1973.

Draeger, Donn F. *The Martial Arts and Ways of Japan, Volume 3: Modern Budo & Bujutsu*. Weatherhill, New York & Tokyo, 1974

Draeger, Donn F. *The Weapons and Fighting Arts of Indonesia*. Charles E. Tuttle Company, Rutland, Vermont, USA, Tokyo, Japan, 1972.

Edelson, Mike. *Cutting with the Medieval Sword: Theory and Application*. CreateSpace Independent Publishing Platform. 2017.

Edelson, Mike. 'HEMA as a Martial Art,' Lecture from Longpoint 2017, https://www.youtube.com/watch?v=9pW4WwN_bM0&index=1&list=PLu6v5wNiTHAXsH6XeN8MauoluxJsoVE9v, accessed April 2018.

Friday, Karl F. 'Kabala in Motion: Kata & Pattern Practice in the Traditional Bugei,' in Skoss, Diane, editor. *Sword and Spirit: Classical Warrior Traditions of Japan, Vol. 2*, Koryu Books, Berkeley Heights NJ, 1997.

Galas, Matt. 'Historical Rule Sets,' HEMA Alliance Forums, http://hemaforums.com/viewtopic.php?t=664. 2010, accessed April 2018.

Galas, Matt. 'Russian Test Cutting Practices,' HROARR Website, http://hroarr.com/article/russia-test-cutting-practices/. 2012, accessed April 2018.

Geißler, Robert. 'Concerning the Dynamics of Swords,' HROARR Website, http://hroarr.com/article/concerning-the-dynamics-of-swords/. 2014 accessed April 2018.

Hull, Jeffrey, with Maziarz, Monika and Żabiński, Grzegorz. *Knightly Dueling: The Fighting Arts of German Chivalry*. Boulder, CO: Paladin Press, 2007.

Jackson, Diedre, *Medieval Women*. The British Library, London, 2015.

Jager, Eric. *The Last Duel: A True Story of Crime, Scandal and Trial by Combat in Medieval France*. Broadway Books, 2005.

Kaeuper, Richard. *Chivalry and Violence in Medieval Europe*. Oxford University Press, Oxford, 1999.

Keely, Liam. 'Interview with Nitta Suzuyo: Headmaster of the Toda-ha Buko-ryu,' in Skoss, Diane, editor. *Keiko Shokon: Classical Warrior Traditions of Japan, Vol. 3*. Koryu Books, Berkeley Heights NJ, 2002.

Keely, Liam. 'The Tojutsu of the Tatsumi-ryu, Murphy's Law and the K.I.S.S. Principle,' in Skoss, Diane, editor. *Sword and Spirit: Classical Warrior Traditions of Japan, Vol. 2*. Koryu Books, Berkeley Heights NJ, 1997.

Lorge, Peter. *Chinese Martial Arts: From Antiquity to the Twenty-First Century*. Cambridge University Press, Cambridge, New York, 2012.

Lowry, Dave, 'Promise and Peril: The Potential of Following Multiple Koryu,' in Skoss, Diane, editor, *Keiko Shokon, Classical Warrior Traditions of Japan*, Vol. 3. Koryu Books. Berkeley Heights NJ, 2002.

Manning, Roger B. *Swordsmen: The Martial Ethos of the Three Kingdoms*. Oxford University Press, Oxford, 2004.

Martens, Krist. 'Towards a New Approach in HEMA Tournaments: Let's Fence Naked!' HROARR website, http://hroarr.com/article/towards-a-new-approach-in-hema-tournaments-lets-fence-naked/. 2014. Accessed April 2018.

Morrison, Susan Signe, *A Medieval Woman's Companion: Women's Lives in the Middle Ages*. Oxbow Books, 2015.

Muhlberger, S. *Jousts and Tournaments: Charny and Chivalric Sport in the Fourteenth Century*. Union City, Calif., The Chivalry Bookshelf, 2003.

Muhlberger, S. *Deeds of Arms: Formal Combats in the Late Fourteenth Century*. Highland Village, TX, The Chivalry Bookshelf, 2005.

Oakeshott, Ewart. *The Archaeology of Weapons*. Dover Publications. New York, New York. 1997 (Originally Published 1960).

Oakeshott, Ewart. *Records of the Medieval Sword*. Boydell Press, Woodbridge, 2002.

Painter, Sidney. *French Chivalry: Chivalric Ideas and Practices in Mediaeval France*. Cornell University Press, Ithaca, 1964.

Ringeck, Sigmund, translated and interpreted by Lindholm, David, illustrated by Peter Svärd, with contributions by Johnsson, Peter, and Strid, Lena. *Sigmund Ringeck's Knightly Art of the Longsword*. Paladin Press, Boulder, 2003 (original text from 1440s).

Ringeck, Sigmund, translated and interpreted by Lindholm, David, illustrated by Peter Svärd, with contributions by Johnsson, Peter, and Strid, Lena. *Sigmund Ringeck's Knightly Arts of Combat*. Paladin Press, Boulder, 2006 (original text from 1440s).

Sieniawski, Bartosz. 'The Saber's Many Travels,' HROARR Website, http://hroarr.com/article/the-sabers-many-travels-the-origins-of-the-cross-cutting-art/. 2013 accessed April 2018.

Skoss, Diane, editor. *Koryu Bujutsu: Classical Warrior Traditions of Japan, Vol. 1*. Koryu Books, Berkeley Heights NJ, 1995.

Skoss, Diane, editor, *Sword and Spirit: Classical Warrior Traditions of Japan, Vol. 2.* Koryu Books, Berkeley Heights NJ, 1997.

Skoss, Diane, editor, *Keiko Shokon: Classical Warrior Traditions of Japan, Vol. 3.* Berkeley Heights NJ, 2002.

Tobler, Christian Henry. *Fighting with the German Longsword.* Wheaton IL, Freelance Academy Press, 2015.

Tobler, Christian Henry. *In Saint George's Name: An Anthology of Medieval German Fighting Arts.* Wheaton, IL, Freelance Academy Press, 2010.

Tobler, Christian Henry. *Secrets of German Medieval Swordsmanship.* Highland Village, TX, Chivalry Bookshelf, 2001

Tracy, Larissa and DeVries, Kelly editors. *Wounds and Wound Repair in Medieval Culture.* Brill, 2015.

Tsuneo, Nishioka. 'Uchidachi & Shidachi,' in Skoss, Diane, editor, *Sword and Spirit: Classical Warrior Traditions of Japan, Vol. 2.* Koryu Books, Berkeley Heights NJ, 1997.

Turner, George. 'Sword Motions and Impacts: An Investigation and Analysis.' ARMA website; 2003, accessed April 2018.

Williams, Allan. *The Knight and the Blast Furnace: A History of the Metallurgy of Armour in the Middle Ages & the Early Modern Period.* Boston, Brill Academic Publishers. 2003.

Vale, J. *Edward III and Chivalry: Chivalric Society and its Context, 1270-1350.* Woodbridge, 1983.

Ward, Jennifer, *Women in Medieval Europe, 1200-1500,* Pearson Education Ltd., 2002.

Weisner-Hanks, Merry E., *Women and Gender in Early Modern Europe,* New Approaches in European History, Cambridge University Press, 3rd ed., 2008.

Zabinski, Grzegorz, Walczak, Bartlomiej. *Codex Wallerstein: A Medieval Fighting Book from the 15th Century on the Longsword, Falchion, Dagger, and Wrestling, (from 1380–1390 & 1450s).* Paladin Press, Boulder; 2002.

Zabinski, Grzegorz. 'Unarmoured Longsword Combat of Master Liechtenauer via Priest Döbringer.' Unpublished revision, 2006.

Index